The Pennine Way

Tony Hopkins

Zymurgy Publishing

Acknowledgements

Anyone writing about the Pennine Way owes a debt first and foremost to Tom Stephenson. His newspaper and magazine articles provided essential background information for me, both for the Pennine Way National Trail guides and for this book. Next, thanks to the family of Bill Fitchett, who lent me his annotated copy of Wainwright's Pennine Way Companion. Uncle Bill was in my thoughts when I was planning this book.

Thanks to John Weatherall for advice in the early days, and for lending me his priceless notebooks. Thanks to Chris Sainty and the Pennine Way Association for sorting out archive photographs and reading the first draft of this book, to Steve Westwood of the Countryside Agency for early support and reading the draft, and to Martin Ellis for being what all publishers should be: enthusiastic, reliable and a little eccentric.

Finally, thanks to Don and Sheila Stokoe and my wife Mary. The four of us shared some magical days on the Pennine Way when I was researching the National Trail guides in the mid '80s; the memories of those days made this project possible.

Design: Nick Ridley
Printed by Compass Press Limited

© Text and Images - Tony Hopkins

First published 2005 by Zymurgy Publishing, Newcastle upon Tyne, United Kingdom

A catalogue record for this book is available from the British Library.

I.S.B.N. 1-903506-13-1

Five minute's sunshine a mile along the way: Upper Booth in early autumn, with mist on the Kinder massif.

The Pennine Way

Contents

Haworth Moor in August; heather and mat-grass on the hilltops, bracken on the slopes of the South Dean Beck.

Introduction

The west face of Kinder, buffeted by icy north winds.

'Stout Shoes Should Be Worn...
With Some Hobnails'

The Pennine Way, Britain's first and most famous long-distance footpath, represents the very best of England's high country and a challenge to body and soul.

Starting at Edale in the Peak National Park, the route crosses the Kinder massif and heads north via Calderdale to the Yorkshire Dales, then up through the Durham Dales and across the Cross Fell range to Alston and the Tyne Gap. It then follows Hadrian's Wall for a few miles before striking north again, over Northumberland's Reiver Country, the Cheviots and the Border Ridge, before a final descent into the Bowmont Valley at Kirk Yetholm. The total distance of the walk is now officially quoted as 256 miles, or 268 miles allowing for the terrain (ie slopes, scrambles and minor detours).

The first leaflet to describe the Pennine Way, published in the mid-1960s and written by trail 'godfather', Tom Stephenson, included sage advice about the special qualities of whipcord breeches and glucose sweets. It assumed that walkers would book their accommodation at farmhouses or Youth Hostels, and that anyone attempting higher ground in bad weather would steer by map and compass. Times have changed. There have been dozens more leaflets and books published down the years. This book grew from my experiences gained when writing the current 'official' Pennine Way guidebooks. Gore-Tex, mobile phones and GIS now make up the modern walkers' lexicon. The route is not as Tom Stephenson would have wished; he thought any surfaced track would be objectionable and preferred the challenge of peat bogs. But all the mountains are still here; the far horizons of the Great Divide.

The adventure starts here: usually before opening time!

'A Way Trodden By Walkers'

Having been born and raised in Derbyshire, I knew the southern Pennines quite well. However, my interests as a teenager in the 1960s were centred around wildlife rather than wild places; I spent most of my spare time bird-watching and rearing moth caterpillars. In my youth the thought of 'hiking' for miles on end, with nothing to show for it at the end of the day, struck me as a perverse waste of time. It was also extremely uncool. Stalking hedgerows with a butterfly net seemed more socially acceptable than going for a ramble in a bobble-hat. My only memory concerning the Pennine Way in the halcyon days of the '60s was when my Uncle Bill Fitchett, a Warwickshire newsagent, made the local newspaper by completing the walk in sixteen days. I liked Bill very much, but could not imagine why he had done it.

top: Featherbed Moss from Mill Hill. How the path looked before the worst sections were stone slabbed.
bottom: Volunteers laying stone slabs on the Border Ridge in Northumberland.

Twenty years later my attitudes had changed. I was living in Northumberland, having followed a career in countryside interpretation, and in 1986 I was asked by the Countryside Commission to write one of the first titles in their new series of National Trail Guides, to the Pennine Way. By then I was familiar with most of the classic northern landscapes and had written several walks books. I had explored the Dales and the Wall country, and was especially fond of Teesdale and the Cheviots. So the task of linking them together and describing a familiar and well-worn route did not seem too much of a challenge.

Work began very slowly. Although I was commissioned by Countryside Commission headquarters at Cheltenham to write both 'Pennine Way North' and 'Pennine Way South', there was some reluctance in their Leeds office to have a guidebook published when the state of the paths and waymarking was far from satisfactory. Both the Yorkshire Dales and Peak National Parks had spent years trying to improve their sections of the Way but arguments persisted about biotex matting and stone slabs. They wanted any guidebook delayed indefinitely. All sorts of other organisations and agencies wanted their say too. Fortunately, things were better in the north. It helped that I worked in the same office as John Weatherall, Northumberland County Council's Footpaths Officer and a veteran of the team who established the route in the early 60s. His advice was of the most helpful kind, explaining where the walked route did not follow the map or the official line, when footbridges were due to be replaced, who I should speak to at Durham about diversions and danger areas. He did not interfere; in retrospect, this was a big help. Thus, when I began to walk sections of the route in February 1988 I was on my own and was able to take things at my own

The beautiful russet and gold of cottongrass in autumn is a sure sign of treacherous ground. The stone slabs make the ascent of Cross Fell relatively easy: it is possible to enjoy the landscape rather than have to wade through peat.

pace. I had separated the northern book into nine parts, and whilst I researched, walked and wrote up the text, Wendy Pettigrew of the Countryside Commission brow-beat everyone into line for Pennine Way South, which was researched and walked in ten parts the following year.

Writing notes whilst walking the Way was as difficult as I had expected it to be. There were dreadful moments when I realised I had missed a junction and would have to retrace my steps for a mile, and even more dreadful moments at my Amstrad computer two or three evenings later when I could not understand my own route description at an essential point and would have to go back to check the fieldwork. It became apparent quite quickly that the official maps were woefully inaccurate and I had to make my own decisions about where the path should be assumed to go; sometimes my text formalised an obvious 'desire line' to avoid bogs, sometimes it pulled the described route back to where it should be on the OS map. It transpired that there was no 'legal' path at all; my notes would constitute the first written route description since Wainwright's questionable classic of 1968, and all the subsequent negotiations and 'alignments' by Countryside Agency and local authority staff have had to take account of the guidebook. This must have confirmed the worst fears of Rights of Way staff who had wanted the route ready for the guidebook rather than the other way round. But at least there has been an incentive for the agencies to fund improvements; without popular use it is possible that the Pennine Way would become just another derelict trail to nowhere.

I finished the Pennine Way fieldwork in the spring of 1989, on Pen-y-ghent with a group of friends and a bottle of champagne. The first book appeared later in that year and although I was proud to have written it I was dissatisfied with the contents.

Autumn in the Cross Fell range: bleached grass and a derelict barn.

Heather

Because it was a user guide the emphasis had been on route description rather than on along-the-way information. What little interpretation I had managed to squeeze in was edited out by the Countryside Commission. Also, because it had to fit the average kagoul pocket the photographs were small and unimpressive. I tried to convince the publisher that there was a place for a 'sketchbook' version of the walk, but nothing came of it.

Over the next few years I revisited sections of the Way to take photographs or check details for new editions, but there were many miles of the route that became lost to me. In 2002/3 I was busy taking a lot of new photographs of the Cheviots, Hadrian's Wall and the North Pennines, and took the opportunity of a guidebook reprint to take a fresh look at the Peak and Calderdale. With new pictures in hand I talked to Martin Ellis of Zymurgy Publishing, who had produced some attractive northern titles and had also (some years ago!) walked the Pennine Way himself. He was enthusiastic and we shared a vision for the project, of celebrating the grandeur of the Pennines, the diversity of landscapes and the exhilaration of being on a famous journey. There would be a big book after all.

As I rewalked sections of the route in the spring of 2004, some for the first time in fifteen years, I found myself smiling at familiar landmarks, touching rock faces and tree trunks and sharing reflective moments with piles of stones on lonely hilltops. When I met walkers carrying a guidebook I smiled and felt absurdly smug with myself. Browsing the internet at home, I found Pennine Way sites with tales posted by walkers, quoting my words

National Trail acorn marker at Cronkley Farm in Teesdale.

in a gesture of complicity. There was something magical about all this: the new book had a space waiting for it on many shelves.

It is interesting to compare how things have changed over the years. On the practical side, the walking surface of the Way is now much better, the notorious boggy bits are stone slabbed and the waymarking is at least adequate. People still enjoy the challenge of the rugged walk from Edale to Yetholm, and are able to do it in a couple of weeks or less if they want to. Perhaps there is now less magic about the British uplands; it has been tamed by familiarity. However, although I have visited many of the world's finest wilderness areas - the Grand Canyon, Damaraland, the Masai Mara and Kakadu - I believe that there is still something special about the English Pennines. I have felt more lost and lonely on Cross Fell than the slopes of Kilimanjaro or Kinabalu. And there is a more dizzying feeling of space on the Border Ridge than on Uluru.

'High Places of Solitude'

There is no doubt that the idea of a long-distance walk along the Pennines had been in the thoughts of many ramblers in the decade following the Great War - a time when access to the countryside was a utopian dream for a generation of city-dwellers who were still living through hard times. The open hills were visible from school and factory windows, and yet ownership of the land was vested in a privileged minority who refused to grant even token access beyond a few limited footpaths. It was in this hostile and politicised atmosphere that an unlikely band of rambler guerrillas planned mass trespasses and demonstrations.

In 1935 the journalist Tom Stephenson wrote an article in the

Mist and mizzle on the gritstone path across Kinder Scout.

13

Daily Herald suggesting a 'Pennine Way' from the Peak to the Border. In 1938 a Pennine Way Association worked the idea into a clear manifesto: 'The wide, health-giving moorlands and high places of solitude… give this route a special character and attractiveness which should be available for all time as a national heritage.' Meanwhile, the Northern Federation of the Ramblers' Association and the Youth Hostels Association researched a potential route and discovered that the 250-mile path contained 180 miles of 'presumed rights of way'; the rest would need to be negotiated every step of the way.

The hostility among landowners, especially in the vital Kinder/Bleaklow area, left no one in doubt that official recognition would take years to achieve. Even existing footpaths were hotly disputed by farmers. Public land-owning agencies lined up to object to having people loose in the countryside. Thus, the British Waterworks Association suggested that the uplands would soon become a 'resort for undesirable characters among whom immorality and licentiousness are rife', and the Commanding Officer of the Rochester Military Camp responded to a polite request by the Ramblers' Association by telling them to go and read the 'Keep Out' notices around the Otterburn Ranges. However, this official belligerence only fuelled public resentment; the pressure for change was irresistible. Recommendations by the Scott Report of 1942, the Dower Report of 1945 and the Hobhouse Report of 1947 all pushed the government towards the creation of National Parks and Long Distance Paths. After the '49 Act a National Parks Commission was charged with submitting proposals for the establishment of long-distance routes, of which the Pennine Way was to be the first. Official approval came in 1951 and there was then a ten-year hiatus whilst all the suggestions/variations/alternatives/proposals and counter-proposals were

Tom Stephenson rallying the troops for a fight against vested interests, landowners and politicians. The Pennine Way was his crowning achievement.
© The Pennine Way Association

sorted out by local authorities at various inquiries.

On 24th April 1965, two thousand people gathered at Malham Moor to celebrate the opening of the Pennine Way. They applauded the fine words of various VIPs, but the real cheer was reserved for Tom Stephenson: pacifist, socialist, campaigning journalist, rambler, visionary. Without him there would have been no 'Hikers' Highway'. It had taken thirty years to realise his dream.

Checking the map on a hot day north of Alston.

Vibrant spring: blue water, green pastures and white rock. Malham Cove in the Yorkshire Dales.

Early sunshine at one of the first gates west of Grinsbrook Booth.

Edale to Crowden

The first and finest long-distance footpath begins at a stile by a walnut tree, a few strides from the Nag's Head in the hamlet of Grindsbrook Booth in Edale.

A walk of any sort starts off with hope and expectation, but it also needs a little luck. The opening stretch of the Pennine Way pitches the walker against the Kinder plateau in Derbyshire's High Peak, a post-industrial honeypot, but capricious and moody. Stories abound of people setting out from the Nag's Head then turning up again a few hours later, demoralised and defeated by appalling weather or impossible terrain. Nobody considers Kinder and Bleaklow to be easy; it is a challenge.

The Booth villages are farming settlements which grew out of summering grounds, where cattle were taken each spring to make the most of open grasslands on the gentle lower slopes of the hills. Eventually the slopes were enclosed as 'intakes' and made into permanent pasture. They are now green and fertile and the first couple of miles of the Pennine Way follows a well-trodden path via Upper Booth and Lee Farm to the steep stone-stepped track called Jacob's Ladder. In the days before railways and trunk roads, the track was a busy trade route between Cheshire and Yorkshire: salt and wool were the main commodities. A packhorse bridge, now a sturdy stone footbridge, marks where enclosed farmland ends and open

moorland begins: Jacob's Ladder is a jaggers' path where the ponies followed a zig-zag path out of the Noe valley onto the hills. A few hundred yards further west there is a pivotal point on the route, where a small medieval stone cross still stands to show the meeting place of three wards of the Royal Forest of the Peak, the hunting preserve of William Peveril. This 'forest' was established in 1068, but like other Norman forests it was not heavily wooded: the designation signified that it was set aside for hunting.

Kinder Scout rises to a respectable 632m (2,088 ft), and most local people choose to call it a mountain. By comparison, Cross Fell is 893m and The Cheviot, 815m. Meanwhile, north and south, Ben Nevis

Linnet

is 1,344m whilst faraway Mont Blanc rises to 4,812m. Height alone tells only part of the story: latitude and location have a significant role. Kinder's reputation rests on its austere beauty, characterised by peat hags, weathered rock outcrops and an uncompromising climate. It can be blowing an ice-laden gale high on the barren black plateau, whilst people are wearing T-shirts in Edale.

In the distant past, about three hundred

Lee Barn Information Shelter, on the climb from Upper Booth to Jacob's Ladder.

An early scare for walkers: mist rolling in from the west and hanging on the crest of Kinder Downfall. Sometimes it clears in a few minutes, sometimes it stays for hours, days...

million years ago, the sandstone that formed Kinder was laid down as sediments dumped in a vast delta. A river system brought sand downstream from the area we now call the Scottish Highlands, and it emptied itself into an equatorial sea, which was rich in plankton, diatoms and shellfish. The organic sediments from the warm sea formed a limy ooze which turned to mud: the further from the coast, the purer the mud. In between the coarse coastal sands and the murky depth of the sea there were silt beds with shifting currents. Eventually, the delta and the sea itself sank in a series of earth movements; a whole new process of delta-building began. In time, this created the coal measures and millstone grit, which covered the Kinder grit to a depth of a mile. Heat and pressure on the original sand, silt and mud worked to create sandstone, shale and limestone.

There was nobody around three hundred million years ago to witness the enormity of these geological events, which is perhaps why it is so hard to get excited about them. It also took a very long time for anything to happen. Eventually, through erosion and a host of ice ages, all the overlying strata were removed, and Kinder was revealed. What had been the coast was now the summit, what had been inshore water were now the mid-slopes and valley-sides, and what had been the muddy depth of the sea was now Castleton and the White Peak. Over the last million years, several more ice ages have come and gone. In many places further north, such as the Cheviot Hills, glaciers smoothed out valleys and changed the shape of the land, but although Kinder was buried beneath half a mile of ice there were no moving glaciers: the well-known clefts, cliffs and rock outcrops

As good as it gets: a beautiful late-winter morning looking to Kinder Scout from Mill Hill in the Peak National Park.

The Kissing Stones, never destined to touch. Bleaklow can be a scary place when the mist hangs low over the plateau. A compass can come in useful: north then west.

North across Torside Reservoir in Longdendale.

were shaped by running water and freeze-thawing in interglacial interludes.

Kinder has craggy good looks, and because it behaves like a mountain it seems churlish not to call it one. Its most spectacular feature is not its summit, which is barren and boggy, but its western edge, overlooking the Sett valley and the Cheshire Plain. The Pennine Way follows this rocky edge north, from Kinder Low to Kinder Outfall , then north-west to Mill Hill. The Downfall is a famous landmark, the place where the River Kinder pitches itself down a dark ravine: sometimes a west wind can cause a blow-back, so that the waterfall defies gravity and the cascade is hurled backwards in confusion: sometimes the waterfall freezes and the rock shelves and boulders become an icicle gallery. Rain falling on Kinder summit either seeps into the Crowden Brook and heads east via the Derwent and the Trent to the Humber, or is gathered to the River Kinder, and flows west via the Sett and the Goyt to the Mersey. One way or another, this landscape is all about water.

After the sharp descent from Kinder's high plateau, to cross the saddle of Ashop Head and arrive on the brow of Mill Hill, the Pennine Way heads for the Snake Pass and has to traverse a sea of peat: the place name Featherbed Moss refers to the deceptively jolly covering of cottongrass. This place used to be a killer, at least to the spirit and ambition of faint-hearted walkers. It also took its toll of the Peak National Park's survey and management teams who experimented for years with geotextile mats and in the end paved the route with stone ('causey') slabs from derelict cotton-mills. The result was a revelation - it allowed people to enjoy the sweeping landscape rather than have to watch where they were wading. The new generation of intrepid Pennine Way walkers is able to save time and energy and arrive at the Snake Pass in good heart. Instead of giving up and turning west down the A57 for the bright lights of Glossop, people are now far more likely to gird their loins and head north for the summit of Bleaklow.

Bleaklow is a brother to Kinder Scout; it shares the same geology, but has turned prematurely bald and has lost its peat cap. This of course is good for walkers, because the gritstone is firm underfoot. After having climbed via more stone slabs and along deep groughs and cloughs, the route loses itself on a wide open summit and uses rock outcrops (the Hern Stones and the Wain Stones) to find its way north again. It is a barren place, inhabited by a few red grouse and mountain hares, and by meadow pipits which are the staple small bird of the uplands.

Perhaps Bleaklow has been diminished as it has become more approachable, but to most people it is still a wilderness, and one of the few places where a compass is more than an affectation. On Bleaklow, no one relies on a GPS unit or a mobile phone.

Icy shadows in Longdendale, but the sun has thawed the pastures above Crowden.

Crowden to Standedge

Gritstone sheep

Packhorses and covered wagons crossed the badlands of the Cheshire Panhandle long before the days of the Wild West. Somehow, the salt-smuggling jaggers of Longdendale have now been forgotten and we have adopted cowboy heroes instead. People are happy to hear about Butch Cassidy's Hole-in-the-Wall Gang, rather than read Alan Garner's gritty and magical tale about Jagger Turner of Thursbitch.

Silk, salt, wool and coal were some of the raw materials transported by packhorses to and fro over the Pennines. Two or three hundred years ago, Longdendale was a famous pinch-point by which goods could be traded between Manchester and South Yorkshire. On the high pass heading east, the map still shows the ghost of a track,

Footbridge on the slope above Crowden Brook.

mostly now lost beneath the A628, linking places like Ironbower Moss, Salters Brook Bridge, Gallows Moss and the Snow Road. What powerful stories this trail could tell!

Longdendale was once a picture of rural tranquillity: a rose between the thorns of the Pennine moors. Crowden was one of its prettiest villages, with its own school and inn as well as a seventeenth-century mansion-house. Then came a turnpike road and a railway line, which required a tunnel to be built, then another railway tunnel, then the River Etherow was dammed and the valley flooded to form a string of reservoirs, then came a marching army of giant electricity pylons and telegraph poles. Manchester's growing demands proved insatiable: the valley quickly fell under the yoke. Even now, in post-industrial torpor, the city calls the tune and uses Longdendale as its playground.

At the foot of the valley is Tintwistle, once a weaving village in the midst of the cotton-mills. Above this is Bottoms Reservoir, then Valehouse, then Rhodeswood, then Torside and finally Woodhead. Together, these five sparkling reservoirs supply Manchester with twenty-four million gallons of water

Cockchafer beetles

a day. But the modern countryside has an amenity value as well as a function. Sailing dinghies pirouette on the wide blue waters of Torside. The railway line is now a footpath, called the Longdendale Trail. Crowden is a Youth Hostel, housed in a rather dull block of what was once a terrace of railway cottages.

Meanwhile, at the head of the valley, Woodhead Chapel stands as a grimy reminder of the price paid: its little graveyard is full of navvies and their families who died in a cholera outbreak during the construction

of the second railway tunnel in 1849.

Having crossed the Etherow via Torside's dam wall and turned north just before Crowden, the Pennine Way climbs out of Longdendale on the shoulder of Crowden Brook, leading to Laddow Rocks, where generations of Manchester rock climbers served their apprenticeship before taking on the great summits of the world. Before very long the rock outcrops peter out and the landscape is back in its livery of black, gold and ochre: the colours of sodden peat. Again, this part of the walk has benefited from the

laying of stone slabs; there is a clear and easy route up and over Black Hill, which used to have an unenviable reputation as the worst few yards on the whole of the Pennine Way.

Stories abound of people getting stuck in the quagmire of Black Hill's dark crown. To some extent, this was a self-fulfilling prophesy based on Wainwright's guidebook of the 1960s, which described the terrain in apocalyptic terms of 'an acid waste' and 'a sea of ooze'. In fact, many walkers get themselves stuck to the waist deliberately so their companions can take photographs of them. Black Hill is a celebrity, a uniquely evil-looking place, but there is no need to wade through slurry and it is often possible to reach the triangulation column at Soldiers' Lump - the only physical feature on the black topping - without getting your underclothes wet.

Black Hill lies on the boundary between Derbyshire and South Yorkshire. It was once in Cheshire and was a landmark for traders, who avoided local taxes by sending their packhorses along the narrow panhandle directly into Yorkshire. At 582m it is not a high hill, but it has earned its dour reputation.

The summit of Black Hill is an awesome sight. It will take more than stone slabs to endear it to walkers, especially those of a nervous disposition.

The Pennine Way crosses the A635 at Wessenden Head. Wessenden used to be a little settlement with a famous pub, the Isle of Skye, but all the buildings were demolished in the 1950s to safeguard the water catchment for nearby reservoirs.

It seems bizarre now, but families in the post-war years were still threatened by epidemics of polio, typhoid and diphtheria. Any potential contamination of the water supply was treated seriously. The loss of the Isle of Skye was a particular blow: the

A635 is still known locally as the Road to the Isles, though a whole generation of travellers will no longer understand why.

The A635 links Holmfirth with Saddleworth; neither is very far away. People caught out by bad weather and requiring accommodation have the choice of turning down or up the road after the descent from Black Hill. Saddleworth still carries grim memories of the Moors Murders, whilst Holmfirth is a comfy little town made famous by 'Last of the Summer Wine'. Whether you love or hate the TV series, the town is full of little cafes (including the one featured on the programme, which makes excellent bacon butties) and is a good place to rest for a day if a blizzard or deluge has set in.

Small and medium-sized reservoirs are dotted all over the South Pennines. Sometimes they are reed-lined and are a home to stoneflies and hawker dragonflies, sometimes they are concrete-edged, and sometimes they are just mud. At migration time - May and September/October wildfowl and waders drop in to rest or feed at the appropriate habitat on their way from coast to coast. Chew Reservoir,

Waiting for the Wrinkled Stocking to open. Holmfirth, a few miles east of the National Trail.

the highest in the country, is well-watched and has turned up rarities over the years like pectoral sandpiper and spotted crake. The Wessenden reservoirs seem to be less attractive for migrants, but in the summer they are visited by breeding waders like curlew, snipe and dunlin. Unfortunately, walkers usually miss them because the birds are wary, only coming to the water's edge early and late in the day; the rest of the time they prefer the cover of heather and moorgrass. The signature species of these high Pennine moors are the golden plover and the twite.

It is surprising how easy it is to walk for a day on the Wessenden/Saddleworth moors and see nothing, except a few sheep, and there are fewer sheep now than there used to be; farmers are encouraged (financially) to decrease their stock, which in turn encourages heather regeneration. The most common sheep breed in the Pennines these days is the Swaledale, which is hardy and can look after itself; it has gained ground at the expense of other local breeds. The Swaledale is horned and has a black face with a white muzzle and (often) white patches around the eyes. In the South Pennines, the Gritstone (which has a mottled face and no horns) is still a common sight too; it has a habit of wandering along the rock outcrops and harassing picnickers for their sandwiches. Until a few years ago all the sheep of the South Pennines were the same colour as the soot-covered rocks, but they have turned several shades lighter with the decrease in atmospheric pollution.

Blackstone Edge, with the black stones gradually losing the soot from a century of dirty rain.

Standedge to Hebden Bridge

Busy roads dissect the Pennines all the way north, but they are particularly thick on the ground between Manchester and Huddersfield. When you are into the rhythm of walking across a lonely upland it is easy to feel smug and superior about people crossing your path, going nowhere fast, on trunk roads and motorways. However, behaving like a bumbling hedgehog when you wander out onto tarmac can have unfortunate consequences. Some of the worst Pennine Way road crossings now have footbridges or even tunnels: the same courtesy afforded to cattle and badgers.

Standedge is famous for its cross-Pennine routes, but only the A62 is above ground. A canal and a railway tunnel run deep beneath your feet. The Huddersfield Narrow Canal Tunnel was opened in 1811 to the strains of 'Rule Britannia' and the cheers of 10,000 spectators. It had no towpath, so when it was in operation the boatmen had to 'leg it' (i.e. lie on their backs and push against the walls or ceiling with their legs). The tunnel was three miles long and it took a narrowboat up to three hours to get from one end to the other. Unfortunately, the canal was never a success and many investors went bankrupt. Eventually, in 1845, it was sold to the Huddersfield and Manchester Railway.

Back above ground, the Industrial Revolution has left a more subtle but pervasive legacy of exploitation and grime on the landscape. Most of the moorland on the Lancashire/Yorkshire border is heavily degraded and is covered in coarse grass rather than heather. Although there is far less atmospheric pollution these days the gritstone edges are still blackened and bare; it will take another decade or two before lichens start to grow again.

A century ago, pretty moorland moths like the grey chi and glaucous shears made use of lichen-covered rocks and dry stone walls as daytime resting places, relying on their intricate wing patterns for camouflage. Industrial pollution changed all that, making the moths all too easily visible to predators. Some species disappeared, others adapted. However, in every population of moths there is variation in wing colour and pattern. Usually, it is the dark ones that stand out on trees or rocks, but when pollution has

Lone walker, ready for anything and in a world of his own. On Standedge, east of Manchester.

blackened the surfaces, the melanic or dark forms have an advantage and there is a natural selection in their favour. In a few years (surprisingly few in some cases) it is the pale form that becomes rare and the melanic form that dominates. Most people have heard of the peppered moth, the textbook example of this sort of industrial melanism, but the process applies to many other species too. Interestingly, the 'normal' (i.e. pale speckled) form of this moth, which was extremely scarce around Manchester in the 1960s, is making a comeback and it is the black form that is getting scarce. Genes never rest.

The Pennine Way keeps closely to the gritstone ridge of the mountain divide, over Moss Moor to the M62, which is crossed via a slim and elegant footbridge. At no point on these moors does the altitude reach 500m, but the distant views give an impression of being on the roof of the world. There is a wonderful airiness, the sharp skyline features risen out of one of the most heavily populated landscapes in Europe. Over the years, Millstone Edge and Blackstone Edge have become places of pilgrimage for the people of Oldham, Milnrow and Littleborough.

Most of the trans-Pennine roads on the Yorkshire/Lancashire border once served as packhorse trails, but it is obvious that some at least were in use long before their heyday in the seventeenth and eighteenth centuries. Travel writers in the eighteenth century, such as Daniel Defoe and Celia Fiennes, described Blackstone Edge as a sort of frontier wilderness, but in fact it must already have been a well-worked landscape, accessible via packhorse causeys and corpse roads. They probably stopped for lunch at the White House Inn, still a popular hostelry on the A58.

The Pennine Way meets one of the most enigmatic of the ancient trackways, north of the main outcrops at Blackstone Edge. This is Dhoul's Pavement, a wagonway of sandstone cobbles and setts, with wheel-grooves and drainage channels. It looks both old and substantial, which must be why it is usually credited to the Romans. In fact the construction work is more likely to have been medieval, but it could have replaced an existing packtrail. At the brow of the ridge, where the 'Roman

Red admiral butterfly

Road' first joins the Pennine Way, there is a small standing stone known as the Aiggin Stone. Again, its purpose is lost in the mists of time but it seems to have been a guidepost or 'stoop' an official marker from the turn of the eighteenth century. There is something companionable about linking up with these enigmatic trails, but there is something spooky about it too; perhaps Dhoul's Pavement was a place for footpads and robbers as well as jaggers and drovers.

After the viewpoint at Light Hazzles Edge the gritstone landscape broadens out and the Pennine Way passes White Holm and Warland Reservoirs (built to provide water for the Rochdale Canal around 1804). It then climbs to Coldwell Hill, overlooking Calderdale, and the whole character of the landscape changes. Gone are the peatland wastes. The open pastures of the upper valleys have been farmed from the Bronze Age and some of the settlements were once 'vaccaries' or cattle ranches, dating back to medieval times.

The heavy clay soils of the Calder valley were never exploited for agriculture; for centuries they were densely wooded and settlements grew up along the terraces. Even in its heyday, farming could not sustain the local population. Instead, most cottagers were involved in textile production, and a dual economy flourished. Affluent 'yeomen-clothiers' put their money into the land,

Standedge, looking southwest to the haze of Oldham and Manchester. Canal and railway tunnels run run deep underground beneath the A62.

The Aiggin Stone, an ancient guidestone at the crest of the cross-Pennine ridge.

Dhoul's Pavement - a medieval cross-border waggonway, but marked on maps as a Roman Road.

but also into wool and worsted. With the profits, they were able to build fine homes, many of which now form the substantial core of settlements like Mankinholes and Heptonstall. Eventually, new machinery made home-based spinning and weaving redundant. Mills opened along the rivers, then steam replaced water power. Families who had been yeoman-clothiers became mill-owners and industrialists, and families who had been cottagers with their own land had to move into terraced houses in overcrowded Hebden Bridge. The Industrial Revolution brought prosperity to some and poverty to many.

More than any other stretch of the Pennine Way, the walk north from Withens Gate on the shoulder of Calderdale reveals how we have created the landscape we deserve: superficially pretty, substantially exploited. There are pastures and bracken-banks, ancient woods and alder groves, derelict barns and renovated mills. Although steeped in history, it owes a lot to the confidence and carelessness of the nineteenth century.

For miles around, and particularly from the Pennine Way, the obelisk of Stoodley

Despite its industrial history Calderdale has some magical woodlands and babbling brooks. North of the Calder the Old Norse influence increases and 'brooks' become 'becks'.

The Rochdale Canal at Hebden Bridge. From satanic mills and grimy canals to Chablis and Saga tours.

Pike sums up the Victorian vision of the countryside: 'sublime' landscapes had to be manipulated: they could not be left to nature.

From the approach to the Pike, on the outpasture of Langfield Moor, Hebden Bridge is tucked away in the valley and there is a last chance to pretend you are in a wilderness. A few minutes later, looking down from the monument, Calderdale is revealed in a jumble of mills and terraces. The contrast is profound.

The 35m high Pike was first built in 1814 as a 'Peace Monument' to commemorate the defeat of Napoleon and the surrender of Paris. There was then an inconvenient delay whilst the French emperor escaped from Elba and rampaged through Europe, but everything was tidied up at Waterloo and the obelisk was completed in 1815. It fell down in 1854 after having been struck by lightning, but local pride insisted it be rebuilt. The present Pike, with some renovation, is as it would have been in the late nineteenth century. It is a key landmark along the Pennine Way, held in affection by almost everyone, but still a megalomaniac blot on the landscape.

Hebden Bridge to Ponden

M ankinholes Youth Hostel, down the steep hill from Withens Gate on the Calderdale Way, is one of the most popular stopovers for people walking the Pennine Way perhaps because it is closer, at the end of a day, than having to go via Stoodley Pike to find a B & B at Hebden Bridge.

For intrepid souls in a hurry the Mankinholes option makes particular sense, because the next day's walk can avoid the detour along the valley into the town. However, for anyone with a day to spare, or weary after a wet crossing of the moors, Hebden Bridge is an astute choice. Not only does it have a high density of restaurants and accommodation, it is also lively and easy

to explore. Everything is fitted into the gorge of the Calder and there are parks and walkways where there were once back alleys to warehouses and fustian mills. The Rochdale Canal sparkles and the double-deck terraces are now luxury dwellings. Gone is the grime, gone is the Hole-in-the-Wall Inn, shut down by the Temperance Association. Hebden Bridge may not be as picaresque as it once was, but when you have walked over 50 miles in a couple of days you probably are not looking for too much excitement.

The Rochdale Canal was a big success in the early years of the nineteenth century. It was well-built and well-managed, and it could outbid and outperform its rivals, the Huddersfield and the Leeds and Liverpool

The steep path north out of Hebden Bridge.

39

Dog gate beside a stile on the track above Higher Underbank. Some dogs are happy to leap fences, others (usually the big ones) have to be carried.

Canals. Along its 33 miles, between Piccadilly Wharf in Manchester and Sowerby Bridge, a total of 92 locks were built, and the majority are still in working order. The stretch of the canal between Todmorden and Hebden is particularly attractive, and its towpath can be used as an alternative Pennine Way route for people who have stayed at Mankinholes and want to pick up the official route again at Charlestown. Although busy with brightly coloured narrowboats, the canal is a good way to see wildlife; the fringes of bur-reed and flag act as a roost for brown hawker and chaser dragonflies, and for blue and azure damselflies. Grey wagtails and kingfishers, herons and dippers, all come and go according to the weather.

On the south side of the valley the canal and river are edged by woodland. Because the hill slopes of Calderdale proved unploughable in the Middle Ages, and unsuitable for later industrial development, the tree cover is almost primeval. Along shady paths it is possible to find flowers like enchanter's nightshade and moschatel, and in spring before the oaks and wych elms are into leaf there are carpets of wood anemone and ramsons.

The north side of the valley is quite different; the slopes face the sun and so any suitable terraces are used for gardens and meadows. Climbing out of Calderdale after an easy night in the town is a shock to the system; the paths are steep. However, after having enjoyed getting off the moors, most walkers are driven by a perverse imperative to get back onto them

Heather spider (Theridium)

The chunky obilisc of the 'Peace Monument' on Stoodley Pike can be seen for miles. Early summer on the north side of Calderdale, with red campion in flower in the foreground.

again. The views are soon excellent Stoodley seems within touching distance to the south, and to the east is the dark tower of Heptonstall Church. Wide open grasslands on the slopes of Clough Head and Standing Stone Hill lead down to the Graining Water, then up again to the small reservoirs at Gorple, Widdop and Walshaw Dean. The place names have a familiar ring to them. It is not always a good idea to squeeze literary associations out of a landscape, but from the Calder to the Worth it is difficult to avoid them.

Heptonstall Moor was the home range of Ted Hughes, a poet of visceral genius who learned about nature from gamekeepers and poachers as well as from teachers. His parents lived at Heptonstall, and he grew up in South Yorkshire. Hughes made his name whilst in Cambridge and America, but the imagery for such poems as 'The Thought-Fox' and 'The Hawk in the Rain' lay in Calderdale. He

Enchanters nightshade

often returned to stay with his parents, and in the late 1950s he and his wife Sylvia Plath explored these moors and sometimes wrote about them. However, Plath was no country girl, and her brilliant 'Ariel' poems owe nothing to this landscape. When Plath committed suicide in the cold winter of 1963, Hughes had her buried at Heptonstall Church, but he never came back here to live; he is buried in Devon. It is an irony that feminist pilgrims have to come to this out-of-the-way place to pay their respects. Her grave is always covered with flowers.

The ground rises steadily after the reservoirs of the Grainger and Alcomden Waters. The Pennine Way arrives at last at Withens via a shallow saddle between Dick Delf Hill and Round Hill. There is something special about the 400m contour; it often signifies a change in the landscape, both physical and spiritual. The vegetation is mainly heather, which means you are back on acidic peat rather than mineral soil. Along the dry path sides, bell-heather is common and makes a bright show of deep mauve flowers in the middle of summer. In the wetter places, cross-leaved heath is a major ingredient in a plant association

A mauve and magenta heather-haze washes over Haworth Moor in August. Cathy and Heathcliffe would have known this view quite well, looking east over South Dean Beck from Top Withins.

A footpath sign directing tourists to Top Withins, the putative Wuthering Heights. Japanese visitors (of which there are many) have their own translation.

(and beyond) comes with literary baggage. The Brontë sisters spent most of their lives here, having been brought up by their poor father (rector of Haworth Church) and a strict aunt. There were six children: the two eldest daughters both

Upper Heights Farm, a popular place to stay on the route of the Way east of Withins. There is a side-path from here leading down to South Dean Beck and the Brontë Waterfalls.

that includes cottongrass, bog asphodel and sundew. Common heather (or ling as it is known in the south) only comes into flower in August, but makes up for it by blanketing whole landscapes. The sweep of moorland from Withens to Haworth is covered in a particularly rich brocade of russet cottongrass, viridian lichen, emerald crowberry and purple heather.

This is Brontë Country, and despite the wide open landscape there is something claustrophobic about it. The heritage industry has done well to package this part of the world as a 'must-see' visitor attraction, but it means that everywhere in the Withens/Ponden/Haworth triangle

Haworth Rectory from the churchyard. An austere building: home to the Brontë family.

'Wuthering Heights' is a breathless tale of love and revenge against a backdrop of swirling mists and lonely farmsteads. Top Withens, a ruin with one of the most glorious views in Yorkshire, is thought to have been the inspiration for the main location. It lies on the Pennine Way but is a disappointment to visit, having been so thoroughly 'conserved' that it looks like a bunker.

Having headed north-east for several miles in the company of ghosts, the Pennine Way turns north and drops down into the Worth Valley at Ponden Reservoir. The route crosses the valley at the foot of the reservoir, but most people detour east to spend the night at Haworth. Although the village is always full of tourists it has plenty of attractions, including the steam railway featured in the film 'The Railway Children'. The old rectory is now a museum. In early spring the churchyard rings to the calls of rooks, nest-building in the tall sycamores.

died in childhood, but the rest (Charlotte, Branwell, Emily and Anne) grew up in a world of their own, creating fantasy heroes and faraway places. In their twenties and thirties all the girls wrote books, of which two (Emily's 'Wuthering Heights' and Charlotte's 'Jane Eyre') have endured and

have been made into films.

None of the Brontës reached the age of forty; their father and Charlotte's husband (the village curate) both survived into their eighties.

It was Emily who seems to have had the spirit of the moors in her veins.

A spring morning at Ponden Reservoir.

Emperor moth, laying eggs on heather. The female flies at night, but the males are diurnal and can be seen dashing over the moors in April and May, tracking down mates via pheromones.

Ponden to Thornton-in-Craven

The middle third of the Pennine Way begins at Ponden Reservoir, west of Haworth. The reservoir is one of the most attractive of hundreds of catch-waters in the area, probably because it is one of the oldest. It was built in 1877 and flooded the confluence of the Ponden Clough Beck and the Worth, creating a promontory for Ponden Hall (the location for 'Thrushcross Grange' in 'Wuthering Heights'). The sheet of water has had over a century to settle into its setting; it looks natural and the reed-beds at its head attract sedge warblers and reed buntings. In winter the open water is good for wildfowl especially diving duck like tufted duck and goldeneye.

Most of the early miles of this stretch of the Pennine Way are across peat, but then the terrain changes and there is an interlude of rolling pastures before limestone makes an appearance. This is an important transition; heather moorland does not reappear for eighty miles.

The Lancashire/Yorkshire boundary runs north/south above Ponden, from Watersheddles to the dome of Bare Hill. Gritstone erratics (dumped here after the retreat of glacial ice) have been incorporated into the ancient boundary, from the Hanging Stone to the Wolf Stones. The Pennine Way follows a sheltered route up Dean Clough, through a network of pastures and finally onto Oakworth Moor. The old trackway and moorland path is edged with bilberry, one of the most important upland shrubs, which is the food

Early purple orchid

47

Step-stile to Dean Fields, at the foot of Ponden Reservoir.

plant of several of the big moorland moths as well as the green hairstreak butterfly.

The green hairstreak is a little jewel of a butterfly, easily overlooked. The male is very territorial and uses favourite perches to watch for intruders; if disturbed it will always circle around and come back to the same place. Green hairstreaks are on the wing in May, and the females lay their eggs on bilberry flowers. In North Yorkshire there is a chance of seeing two relatives of the hairstreak on the wing in early summer, the small copper and the common blue. They prefer grassy habitats (the food plants are dock and trefoil) but they like the south-facing slopes of moor edges, where they can sunbathe.

The purple/black fruits of bilberries are a

Green hairstreak butterfly

Cow parsley and buttercups grace the green, highly-fertilized fields near Middleton, north of Ickornshaw.

favourite food for blackbirds and grouse. If you are lucky and can get to them first, they also make the best pies in the world. There are very few other foods for free on the moors, crowberries and cowberries look a lot nicer than they taste. In some boggy places, cranberries occur but they are not the same species as the American sauce-making cranberry.

Ickornshaw Moor is the last of the peatland crossings until north of the Stainmore Gap. It used to be a nasty wet place and it still is, apart from the path which has been greatly improved in recent years. Unusually, the moorland here is classified as common land; most grouse moorland is owned and managed by estates, who can afford the expense of

Flowers of dog-rose are beautiful and transient. The blossom only lasts a few days in June: for the rest of the year there are thorns.

keepering, but for centuries this moor has been run by the 'Shooters' of the Cowling Gun Club. For many years a character called Lot Shuttleworth looked after the management for the Shooters, for which he received a few cartridges as payment.

Moors that are managed for grouse are usually good for wildlife too because the mix of different-aged heather creates a variety of habitats, and because predators such as foxes are controlled. It will be interesting to see if increased public access to the moors in future has an effect on wildlife. Birds of prey like hen harriers are likely to increase (because of better control of illegal poisoning etc.), whilst waders like the curlew are likely to find any disturbance unacceptable. There is no easy solution to the vexed question of how heather moorland should be managed; it is an artificial habitat and what benefits one species may not benefit another.

Down from the open commons the Pennine Way picks its way beside dry stone walls and hawthorn hedges, the intake and enclosure landscape of the eighteenth and nineteenth centuries. Cowling and its neighbouring hamlets of Middleton and Ickornshaw are farming settlements, built around a spring or stream in a patchwork of fields. Once upon a time this was grain-growing country, but stock-rearing became an easier option with the expansion of the mill towns (which had to be fed). Most families who lived here in the eighteenth century spent half their lives tending cattle and the other half weaving on hand looms. They were not affluent times. Early in the nineteenth century the Napoleonic Wars made rich men out of local landowners, who spent their money building follies like the 'Salt and Pepperpot' towers on the hills to the east of the village. In this part of the world very little money went into agrarian innovation.

The high enclosed pastures of Lothersdale rise at last to Pinhaw Beacon, from where there is one of the best panoramic views in the

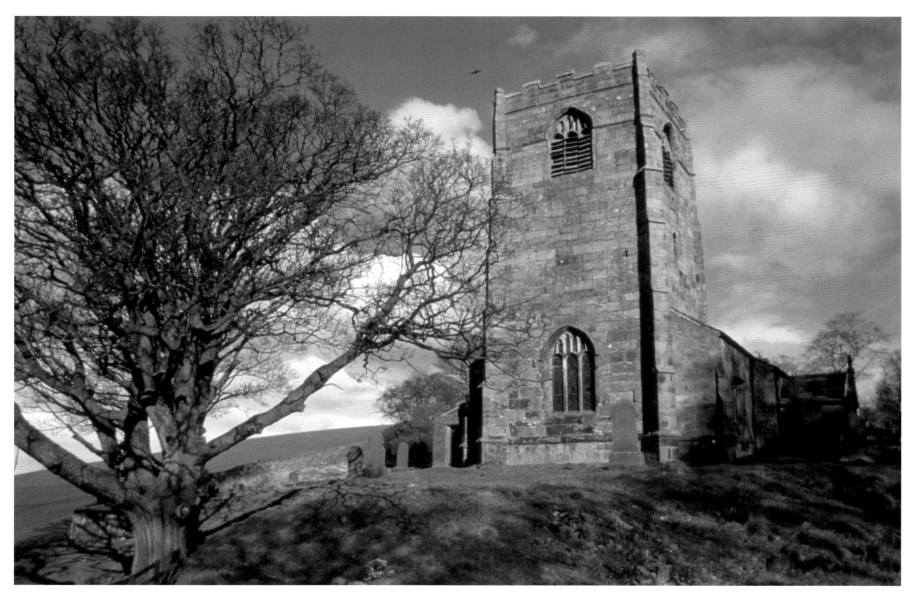

Thornton Church in March: snowdrops in the graveyard and rooks around the tower.

Pennines, particularly considering the modest altitude. Pendle Hill claims special attention, as it always seems to do, even from afar. As well as being famous for witches, Pendle Hill was an inspiration for George Fox, founder of the Quaker Movement. He climbed it in 1652 and "saw the sea bordering upon Lancashire. From the top of this hill the Lord let me see in what places he had a great people to be gathered." Meanwhile, far to the north, Pen-y-ghent also catches the eye, because it is beautiful.

Brown-lipped snail

Robin nest in an old hawthorn stump.

Thornton-in-Craven to Malham

Before the Pennine Way gets into its stride in the Yorkshire Dales it has a quiet interlude of pastures and waterside walks north of the village of Thornton. Most of the settlements in this part of the Craven District are small and lie on ancient cross-Pennine trails. There are mesolithic sites in the area where hunter-gatherers established temporary camps as they followed herds of deer and wild cattle through the ash forests. Only a few excavated microliths (small flint blades) survive to hint at a way of life that survived for thousands of years, before the late Neolithic and Bronze Ages when people settled down to clear the land for farming. Apart from prehistoric mysteries, Thornton also has a role in Roman history; there was a fort at nearby

Morning sunshine on the cottage terrace, north out of Thornton-in-Craven.

'Double-decker' canal bridge near East Marton. The upper arch was a late addition, built to raise the level of the A57 trunk road.

Elslack and a Roman road runs through the village, heading due west as the A56 turns south for Colne. Villages often hide more than they reveal, and rarely share their secrets.

Deep shady lanes lead into Thornton from the north and south. They have a medieval look about them, and lead to nowhere in particular. The Pennine Way makes clever use of the lanes in and out of the village, and they reveal the valley in a different light, of green shadows and dappled celandine banks. Once over the pastures to the north, everything changes again and the route meets the towpath of the Leeds and Liverpool Canal.

Having flirted with two failed canals already, the attractive Leeds and Liverpool Canal has a different story to tell, and for once the Pennine Way stays with it for a little while. Whilst the Rochdale and Huddersfield canals were both sold off to the railway in the middle of the nineteenth centuries, this line kept going as a commercial operation until 1964. It was the first trans-Pennine canal to be started and

the last to be finished. It runs for 127 miles, making it the longest in the country, and in the nineteenth century it made a steady profit carrying wool, limestone and coal. It is now managed by British Waterways; it costs over two million pounds a year to maintain, and attracts about twelve million visitors to see its most famous features Wigan Pier, the Burnley Embankment and the Foulridge Tunnel.

Between Thornton and Gargrave the canal is pretty rather than dramatic. There is one unusual structure, a 'double-decker' bridge at East Marton, but the main characteristic of the canal is that its locks are grouped into flights and there are relatively few cuttings, so there are long sections which follow contours rather than slicing through hillsides. Graceful curves and uncluttered towpaths are thus a feature of the Leeds and Liverpool Canal, and it is a pleasure to keep company with it.

Willow trees (osier, cricket-bat willow and sallow) often line the banks. They provide a food plant for several species of moths, such as the puss moth,

A venerable crab-apple tree, south of Gargrave.

Footprints on the river bank, of oystercatcher, mallard and mink. The oystercatcher has been probing for worms or moluscs.

The most beautiful riverside walk along the Pennine Way: the Aire north of Newfield Bridge.

Snow in the shadows: Town Head at Malham in the Yorkshire Dales.

pebble prominent and poplar hawk. Although nocturnal, these impressive creatures can often be seen sitting on tree-trunks and fence-posts. Willow seems to be a countryside alternative for these moth species - near towns they prefer poplar. Some canalside willows are pollards, their branches lopped every few years to be used for fencing or firewood. Pollarding may increase the life expectancy of a tree from a hundred years to a thousand.

The canal water is an important wildlife habitat, because it does not flood or dry up and it is usually edged with semi-aquatic vegetation. Water voles have always been associated with canals and are still to be found here, though their numbers have declined dramatically due to the ease with which they can be caught by mink. Vole 'gardens' of grazed vegetation close to the water's edge are a give-away to their presence. Voles are neither shy nor nocturnal and can sometimes be seen swimming from one bank to another, like miniature beavers.

By the time the Pennine Way reaches Gargrave it has left the canal two or three fields to the west, where it is carried via an aqueduct over the River Aire. Apart from when it is crossed just north of the village, this will be the last encounter with a canal, a sign that the industrial South Pennines has been left behind.

Gargrave is another village on an important trans-Pennine route, the Aire Gap. For walkers, the most attractive feature is probably the famous Dalesman's Cafe, on the corner of the village square. After a cup of tea it is worth wandering along the river, where there are seats to admire the bridge and watch children playing around the buttertub stepping stones. Butterbur, a plant with big rhubarb-shaped leaves, lines the bank and would once have been used to wrap butter in the local farms. This part of Yorkshire is cattle country; there used to be big herds of shorthorns and Freisians, but the dairy industry is in terminal decline and you can walk for hours without even seeing a Holstein. What cattle there are (sucklers etc.) are inwintered and are only encountered in the fields from April to November.

North of Gargrave, the Pennine Way

Meadow ants carrying a grub to a new nursery chamber, just below the surface of the ant-hill.

enters the Yorkshire Dales National Park. The route leads across rolling pasture to Newfield Bridge, then past an old quarry to Newfield Laithe (a 'laithe' is a barn) and then via Kiln Hill to Airton, on the River Aire. As usual, map features and place names provide clues about land use. The abundance of ash trees indicates that the bedrock here is limestone, but it is dark grey and buried beneath glacial drift and shale. There are several small quarries in the area, worked in the last century to provide building stone or limestone for burning in kilns, to produce slaked lime for use as fertiliser or for mortar. Local or vernacular buildings reflect the raw materials to hand, which adds to the variety and character of the countryside.

The River Aire is a delight, and the wander along its grassy bank north towards Malham contrasts with days spent tracing the peat runnels of the Peak. Gills, sykes and becks bring sparkling water down off the green hills, but because shale and limestone is free-draining the ground is rarely waterlogged. Dissolved calcium is suddenly abundant, which means creatures like molluscs and crustaceans can flourish. In the water there are freshwater mussels and crayfish, whilst under the bushes there are brown-lipped snails and pill-woodlice.

Several of the buildings close to the river are old mills of one sort or another. In this part of Yorkshire most farming families in the 1800s sent their sons and daughters to work in the cottonmills. There was more to labour than clogs and cloth caps - people endured long hours for poor pay then died of TB and byssinosus. Their descendants probably work in the heritage industry.

Malham is a tourist honeypot and after a day in peaceful countryside it comes as a surprise to find yourself walking along a road lined with parked cars. The National Park Authority does its best to keep the village uncluttered and attractive, but of course, that just encourages more people. A National Park Visitor Centre selling ice cream adds to the mêlêe. The National Park logo, the face of a Swaledale ram, looms large on signs and notices. Of all the logos of all the National Parks, this one is probably the most recognisable and effective, though the Swaledale breed is now so universal that it could represent almost any other Park, except perhaps the Broads and the South Downs.

Why the Swaledale has become such a popular sheep breed is open to question. Most of its attributes are shared by the Scotch Blackface, which is decreasing in numbers even on its native heather. Swaledales are hardy and need little shepherding, and they also make good mothers. When put to a Blue-faced Leicester tup they produce a 'mule' lamb ideal for fattening on lower pastures. On the other hand, they are just about the least intelligent of creatures, and their greatest skill is to be able to climb dry stone walls which therefore require unsightly fencing.

Drystone walls lattice the pastures on the east bank of Malham Beck.

Malham to Horton in Ribblesdale

The best way to appreciate awesome views is to have earned them. Most of the life-enhancing moments on the Pennine Way come after a hard walk. Not so the splendours of Malham Cove; a gentle stroll wins all.

Some people like to make the most of their introduction to the Dales landscape by adding a detour to their itinerary, stopping for afternoon tea at Malham before heading east for a mile to Gordale Scar, where there is a famous gorge and a much-photographed waterfall. Others prefer the attractions of a busy pub or an early night. Whatever the choice, the day's walk north of Malham is likely to be a highlight of the National Trail; everyone remembers Pen-y-ghent.

Goldfinch

Purple Saxifrage

Yorkshire's Great Scar Limestone was laid down in the equatorial seas of the carboniferous period. Malham sits at its southern boundary, where coral reefs once divided deep water from shallow lagoons. After a series of earthquakes the land was squeezed and buckled until the bedrock cracked; strata slid under and over to relieve the pressure, leaving fault-lines. Mountains were thrown up, only to be smoothed over by desert winds and ice ages. The great amphitheatre of Malham Cove is where the solid rock just above the Middle Craven Fault was eroded back to create a dazzling cliff of limestone, over which a Niagara-sized waterfall flowed. Eventually, the river dissolved a channel into the limestone north of the Cove and disappeared underground. Today, the walk up from Malham village follows the ancient river bed; what was a cauldron has been replaced by a tinkling stream.

Having followed the easy path to the foot of the Cove, the Pennine Way has to find a route up. Climbers enjoy the challenge of a vertical ascent of the sheer cliff, but for everyone else there is a steep boulder-strewn path west and north, onto a platform of bare rock. From here the landscape looks primeval and spare, weathered to its bones. This is a 'karst' landscape, a world of bleached grey sediments and dry screes, created by rainwater dissolving the limestone bedrock. Ice has had its part to play too, shattering and scouring the surfaces so that everything is smoothed off and topped by debris. Soil is thin because any organic matter is washed away; plants have to fight for a footing, for water and for nutrients.

The platform or plate of bare pockmarked rock on the lip of Malham Cove is an example of limestone pavement, a bizarre land form made up of flat blocks or clints and deep fissures or grikes. Shrubs and herbs often crowd the fissures, their roots thrust deep into crevices to seek out water, and their flowers and foliage reaching out to the sunshine. Limestone pavement is not as common as it should be; where accessible it has been stripped away to be used for garden walling and rockeries. Most of what remains, in the uplands of Yorkshire, Lancashire and Cumbria, is protected within nature reserves. Malham Cove's

One of the Dale's iconic treasures, Malham Cove. A great waterfall once plunged down the sheer limestone cliff. These days Malham Beck issues from an underground cavern and the cliff is the haunt of jackdaws and rock-climbers.

pavement is not one of the best examples, because for centuries it has been grazed by sheep, which clip off all vegetation at ground level. It is fascinating to look down into the grikes and see plants such as dog's mercury, primrose and bloody cranesbill growing in their own hidden microhabitats.

The Pennine Way follows Ing Scar north over a brow at Comb Hill and Dean Moor, then past Water Sinks, where Malham Beck disappears underground. Malham Tarn is over the next brow to the north. This landscape has a well-tamed look to it. There are prehistoric settlements around Comb Hill, suggesting people once exploited fish and wildfowl from the tarn, and good grazing land for deer and

Dog's mercury

Whitebeam and ash find a foothold on the crumbling limestone on the lip of Malham Cove.
Looking south and south-west, over Ribblesdale to Pendle Hill.

livestock. In Norman times this land was owned by William Percy (of Northumberland), who gave it to the Cistercian monks of Fountains Abbey. They made a lot of money from grazing sheep and stocking the tarn with trout. So it has always been a comfortable place, and it is no coincidence that Malham Moor was where the great and the good (ministers, celebrities and national press) were invited for the official opening of the Pennine Way in 1965.

The setting of Malham Tarn looks contrived, and although the lake is natural (formed over a glaciated basin with slate bedrock) it was enlarged and prettified around 1791 when Lord Ribblesdale built his 'shooting lodge' here. The lodge or mansion is now owned by the National Trust and is leased to the Field Studies Council, who run it as a Field Centre. The tarn is managed as a nature reserve, of special interest because its water is eutrophic or nutrient-rich.

Away from the cosiness of Malham, one of the real attractions of the limestone plateau and high hills of North Yorkshire is the feeling of being in a big country, with far horizons and shimmering skies. Great Scar Limestone forms the tableland, but now this is topped by a thick band of what is called the Yoredale Series, more limestone, but with bands of sandstone and shale. A score of hills between Malham and Hawes top 600m, and the highest, Whernside, is a respectable 736m. Even so, from a distance it is Ingleborough and Pen-y-ghent that catch the eye. They look magnificent, with a profile reminiscent of the great mesas of the Utah badlands. Beneath a flat cap of millstone grit there are layers of limestone and terraces or steps of shale, then steep walls of limestone and more eroded shale and sandstone, then the level base of the Great Scar. It would be inconceivable for the Pennine Way not to embrace one or other of these

Swaledale sheep on Malham Moor.

Buttercup meadows and green pastures, with Pen-y-ghent in the background.

Pen-y-ghent's cliffs, out of reach of sheep, provide a refuge for classic 'calcicole' or lime-loving plants like rockrose and spleenwort. Even the redoubtable Wainwright noticed the profusion of purple saxifrage on the western ramparts of the hill, 'like aubretia on a garden wall'. However, the summit (at 694m) is no more than a scatter of gritstone boulders, and the rocks around the cairn are often decorated by little piles of orange peel or other flotsam. The only comfortable place for a picnic is the S-shaped shelter built into the wall as part of the National Park's fiftieth anniversary in 2004. On the whole, this place is too popular for its own good.

There is always something special about the last leg of a journey. Having earned the views and turned for home, the Pennine Way descends steeply from Pen-y-ghent; Ribblesdale and the white flanks of Ingleborough lie in front of you and a green road angles south-west to carry you down into the homely village of Horton.

magical hills, and with a little ingenuity the route has been tweaked west to create a zig-zag or dog-tooth over Fountains Fell, then north to Pen-y-ghent.

For many people, the sharp climb up Pen-y-ghent and the exhilaration of being at the top of the world at just 694m is a highlight of the whole Pennine Way.

There is often a mist on the slopes or on the summit, but this rarely blots out all the views and there is something both surreal and serene about getting above the clouds and looking across a white sea to the floating tabletop of Ingleborough, and to Pendle Hill and Bowland and the far Howgills.

Horton in Ribblesdale to Hawes

Peacock butterfly

All the way from Fountains Fell to Horton in Ribblesdale the limestone of the Great Scar is being eaten away by the carbon dioxide in rainwater. This has been happening for millions of years (acid rain is not a new phenomenon) and maps of the area are covered with epithets like 'shake', 'sink' and 'swallow' holes. Clearly, rainwater does not only dissolve surface rock; it has hollowed out such a network of subterranean tunnels and chambers that any cross-section of the Yorkshire Dales would look like a slice of Gruyere cheese. So as well as walkers, cyclists and horse-riders on the paths and bridleways, and hang-gliders on thermals, there are potholers underground trying to explore such dark labyrinths as the Long Churn and Alum Pot.

The walled track north-east from Horton, with Ribblesdale to the left and the open fells of Pen-y-ghent rising to the right.

There are all sorts of ways to enjoy a day in the great outdoors. The Dales are full of people seeking solitude and a challenge, and it is interesting to gather at places like the Crown Hotel or the Pen-y-ghent Cafe in Horton and listen to their stories. As well as its Pennine Way connections, Horton marks the start and end of the Three Peaks Challenge, the twenty-six mile walk linking the three big hills of Whernside, Ingleborough and Pen-y-ghent. This bracing (sometimes lethal) walk is considered a rite of passage for anyone with Yorkshire blood in their veins. Hence, the village is always busy, and although there are pubs and hotels as well as a campsite, accommodation can be a problem.

Horton has medieval origins, and St Oswald's Church even has some Romanesque features. Most of the land was in the hands of the three abbeys, Furness, Fountains and Jervaulx, who were interested in farm rents and sheep husbandry. However, the village really came to life in the nineteenth century, as a stopping place on the Settle to Carlisle Railway and the nearest focal point for a clutch of limestone quarries. Unlike other flash-in-the-pan settlements, Horton has survived with the same economic lifelines, there are still big roadstone quarries eating into Ribblesdale and the Settle to Carlisle Line is now a tourist attraction. But without benighted walkers the village would lose its lifeblood.

The Pennine Way heads purposefully out of Horton along a handsome walled track as far as Sell Gill Holes. This is one of the most popular potholes in the area and there are often cavers about to explain what they are doing and why. The entrance to the

Ribblehead Viaduct. A ride on the Settle-Carlisle Railway is an excellent way to enjoy the Dales landscape, but the arches can only be viewed properly from a footpath. The Pennine Way runs a mile or two to the east.

cave system is to the east of the path; below your feet, intrepid cavers (usually students) may be exploring the black clammy depth of a rift chamber a hundred metres down. A little further along is Jackdaw Hole and Long Churn, whilst across the valley to the west of Selside is Alum Pot, one of the most impressive of the Yorkshire caves. In 1781, the Rev John Hutton described this as a 'terrible hiatus, which caused such a dreadful gloom from the spray it raised up as to make us shrink back with horrour.' The language may seem quaint but looking down into potholes can be quite unsettling.

Back on *terra firma*, the landscape takes on an unearthly pallor as limestone terraces and screes dominate both sides of the Ribble. There are wonderful shelves of limestone pavements just off the route, and springs and flushes where wood cranesbill and marsh orchid turn the slopes mauve and magenta. At Ling Gill there is a deep gorge where ash woodland has survived since late-glacial times, and where wood warblers and redstarts call from the canopy.

But all the while, the path is seeking the high ground and the way north and east. Land forms change, features recede and you feel smaller and smaller in the vast emptiness of Gayle Moor and Cam Fell. There seems to be no foreground at all: everything is pushed back to the horizon. Even Ribblehead Viaduct, one of the most famous icons of the age of steam, looks as if it was made by Hornby. Underfoot there are sudden depressions in the turf called shake holes, where boulder clay (the

thick layer of fine debris dumped by glaciers after the last Ice Age) has been washed into fissures in the Yoredale limestone. Close by on the slope to the east, and below the recent conifer plantations at Cam Pasture, there are old quarry workings where millstone grit was worked, to be used in farmhouse window frames and lintels back in Horton.

Cam High Road is marked on maps as a Roman Road but it certainly seems older. It is also muddy and rutted and is used by motorbikes and ATVs. Nothing irritates walkers more than having to share a path with internal combustion engines. Horses and mountain bikes are bad enough, but as least they do not whine and smoke. However, the Pennine Way and the Dales Way, which coincide here for a few miles, are latecomers and it is best to be pragmatic about the state of the track. As well as Roman soldiers and their provisions, this ancient thoroughfare was used to drove cattle and packhorse trains

Common blue butterflies on bird's-foot trefoil.

on the medieval wool trail. It has probably been a broad muddy furrow in the wilderness for three thousand years, and it resembles nothing so much as the Vladimirk Road to Siberia, as painted by Isaak Levitan. Of all the ancient ways picked up and discarded by the Pennine Way, this is the one that broods about its past and whispers to lonely travellers.

Cam High Road leads to West Cam Road and more shake holes on the shoulder of desolate Dodd Fell. There is nothing easy about this landscape; it does not cater for after-lunch leg-stretchers. Which makes it all the more surprising when the boggy path turns into a green lane and the airy tops transmute into a patchwork of walled pastures and meadows. This sudden pastoral idyll is Wensleydale (old Yoredale: the valley of the Ure) and it is nearly time for tea and scones.

Hawes is known as the 'Capital of Upper Wensleydale', but the truth is that there is little competition for the title. In the twelfth century the whole upper valley was a royal forest, reserved for hunting, but like Horton it was then passed to the local monasteries, who traded in wool and made cheese. When the monasteries were crushed by Henry VIII, sheep rearing continued, and almost every home in the town was employed to spin and knit. The settlement was granted its market charter in 1699, and it still has its own mart where locally reared sheep and cattle are sold.

So although Hawes is one of the busiest tourist towns in the Dales, it has not entirely sold its soul. Apart from tea and scones, the main attractions are the Dales Countryside Museum (housed in the old railway station) and the 'Cheese Experience' at the Wensleydale Creamery.

Hawes Railway Station: the Dales in aspic.

Sweet Cicely, like cow parsley but with lush aniseed-scented foliage, lines the path close to the Haylands Bridge over the River Ure, north of Hawes.

Hawes to Keld

Dipper

Wensleydale is arguably the prettiest of the Yorkshire Dales and the most accessible, which makes it a place to avoid at busy times of the year. The broad valley cradles the River Ure, etched into the limestone bedrock. Deep underground there is a much older foundation of hard rock called the Askrigg Block, a contorted mass of shale and sandstone with a big lump of granite wedged into it, which was pushed up as molten lava in some unimaginable earth movements about four hundred million years ago. This granite now lies five hundred metres beneath the surface, under the limestone sediments, and has only ever seen the light of day in a borehole sample. Geologists try hard to excite our imagination about how the landscape was created, but without an eyewitness it is impossible to credit gentle Wensleydale with such a violent past.

The River Ure meanders through pastures and meadows, and its tributaries cut into steep slopes north and south. Waterfalls tumble from limestone cliffs, beneath which shale and sandstone has been eroded and scooped back to create overhangs and plunge-pools. The most impressive of the Dale's waterfalls is Hardraw Force, just off the Pennine Way but easily visited via the Green Dragon Inn. Like other famous falls, everything at Hardraw depends on how much rain has been gathered in the hills a day or two earlier; the spectacular thirty metre vertical chute of Hardraw is often about as fierce as a bathroom shower.

Most of Wensleydale's streams flow over shelves of limestone, often in sequences that create dramatic little torrents and cataracts. Wildlife is sometimes prolific, so that on lucky days, morning and evening, you may see a kingfisher, goosander or water shrew hunting in the clear waters. Everything depends on the availability of aquatic life, fish and invertebrates.

Mayflies and caddis flies, stoneflies and alderflies, are all aquatic in their early stages and they rely on a current of water to flush nutrients downstream, to supply them with enough dissolved oxygen to breathe. When the becks are low in warm weather the water becomes sluggish and the invertebrates suffer. Thus most

On the causey path out of Hawes in Wensleydale, through Haylands with the high fells ahead.

mayflies and stoneflies are on the wing in the spring, and caddis flies are most active in the autumn. Birds fit their breeding season around the invertebrate cycle, dippers nest very early to be able to feed their young on full-grown aquatic larvae, whilst grey wagtails wait and harvest the winged adults. Meanwhile, trout and crayfish have to sit out floods and droughts and keep to the kelds or deeper pools when the shallows are dry. So what you see along a stream or river depends on things you cannot see in the water. Waterfalls and torrents aerate water and add oxygen, farm run-off removes it. The Ure is in a much better state now than it was a few decades ago.

The walk north from Hawes begins by crossing the flat valley-bottom to meet a bend in the river, but to get there it follows a causey path across a green meadow, past a stone barn; a pretty sight against the curtain of high hills from Great Shunner to Abbotside. This is a sample of the classic walls/fields/barns landscape of the Yorkshire Dales. The farming system that created it was geared towards cattle-rearing; fields were cut for hay in the middle of summer when the stock was away on the outbye, and hay was then stacked in the barn lofts to feed the beasts in the winter. It was a very efficient way of farming on a small scale, but only when labour was cheap. A few head of cattle took a lot of care and attention, and when mechanisation arrived there was no way for most farmers to make a living without amalgamation and capital investment.

Centuries of hay production created meadows brimming with wild flowers: a happy accident of grass production. Farmers spread muck over their fields and then left the crop to grow and seed in mid to late summer, when the cut was taken. Since then, intensive farming in most of Britain has resulted in the sowing of 'better' grass mixes, which are fertilised with inorganic nitrogen and cut in early summer. Instead of having to wait for good weather to dry

Haylands Bridge, over the river Ure in Wensleydale. The clints of Abbotside Common on the skyline.

the hay, farmers make silage, which can be stored in clamps or bagged wet.

The Dales meadows survive today because farmers are encouraged by government schemes to manage their land traditionally, to maintain the sort of countryside National Park visitors want to see. Walking through fields full of buttercup, hayrattle, eyebright, sorrel, cranesbill and marsh orchid is one of the great joys of the Pennine Way. But it is only a joy in June and July. Once the hay has been cut, and then until May of the following year, old meadows are no prettier than grass leys or pastures. The

Placing a stone on the cairn: Great Shunner Fell on a hazy still day.

on the morning walk out of Hawes and Wensleydale, then later in the day on the descent into Swaledale and the village of Thwaite. In June, the meadows of Kisdon Hill are a blaze of gold, peppered white and red and purple. A month or so later the colours are gone. So for a few days there is the sound of tractors and balers with the heavy scent of the hay as it is led and stacked. There is something very special about being out in the countryside when it is yielding its harvest.

One of the problems about taking on the Pennine Way is deciding on the best time of year. Clearly, the Dales valleys are at their best in early to mid summer, but this is not true of the plateau uplands. Between Hawes and Thwaite the route climbs a long grassy ridge to Hearne Top, then to Hearne Head and to Great Shunner Fell at 716m. In the autumn this can be a glorious place of silver-green pastures capped by russet moorland, with crisp sunlight and faraway views. But in summer the landscape can be a tedious green, its views flattened by haze and a high sun. There is no easy solution to the dilemma, except to do the walk twice!

barns that were an integral part of the system are now a liability for landowners and the National Park Authority; nobody can afford to maintain them and they have no useful purpose. Many have disappeared, dismantled for their stonework. Of all Pennine landscapes, the meadow systems of the Yorkshire and Durham Dales are the most fragile. Their long-term future is far from secure.

Some of the most picturesque barns to have survived the cull are to be seen

Great Shunner Fell from Wensleydale. Early on a midsummer morning, with the hillsides flat green and drying fast.

Kisdon Hill, at Thwaite in Swaledale. Over the years the lower fields have been lost to bracken through overgrazing. Sheep were the salvation and ruination of the British uplands. Now farmers are encouraged to reduce flock sizes.

Keld to Bowes

The River Swale, above Keld

Keld is one of the nicest places to stay on the Pennine Way. There is nothing special to do and nowhere special to go, except to idle away an hour at the leafy bower of Kisdon Force. But, after a long day on the trail, that is quite enough. Keld has a Youth Hostel and excellent B & B facilities; after tea it is good to sit beside the Swale and watch the dippers as they bob from stone to stone. People pass south-north or east-west (on the Coast to Coast walk), so there is always someone to gossip with about the weather. Nothing else matters.

Civilisations come and go, but in the uplands place names endure. This may be because there are no better alternatives. When Norse settlers first explored the Dales' rivers and settled to make their home here (in the Dark Ages), they applied their own descriptive names to features they were familiar with, especially to do with water. Thus a rake or path might follow a sike or small stream as it descended via a gill or ravine to a beck or stream, which might then flow past a lathe or barn in a thwaite or clearing via a keld or deep patch of water to a force or waterfall. All these words are still used both to describe particular landscape features and as elements in place names. Later, English (or Yorkshire) farmers added their own words to distinguish more esoteric features like woods and rock outcrops, as in High Frith and Hind Hole. All of this

Kisdon Force, at Keld in Upper Swaledale. The ice is thawing fast on a sunny April morning.

helps to explain the delightful place names employed along the upper Swale around Keld, such as Birk Hill, where birches grew, and Catrake Force, a waterfall by the path leading to where wildcats once had a den. Some names are prosaic, as in Coalpit Hill; others are mysterious, as in Palla Nears. By reading the names on a map it is often possible to piece together a vivid picture of what may seem an ordinary place. Of course, nothing explains how Crackpot Hall (above the confluence of the Swinner Gill) earned its sobriquet.

The Swaledale/Stonesdale valley is the last chance to enjoy the meadow landscape of the Yorkshire Dales. By the time Stonesdale has changed to Startindale the Pennine Way is heading for the high moors, north-east and out of the National Park. The path follows a packhorse trail, at its busiest in the lead-mining bonanza of the early nineteenth century when there were mines extracting galena all the way up Swaledale.

Over the rise of Lad Gill Hill on Stonesdale Moor, the windswept expanse of moorland is littered with shafts and rubble from long-forgotten coal mines associated with

Tan Hill Inn, its reputation rests with the weather: the colder the day, the warmer the welcome.

The River Greta above God's Bridge, near Bowes in County Durham. Midwinter, but it could as easily be mid-spring: the weather is capricious in the northern hills.

the Tan Hill Colliery. The mining traditions here are more to do with the Durham Coalfield than with Yorkshire; there are old workings reminiscent of pockmarked Cockfield Fell near Barnard Castle, where coal was extracted for several hundred years. In the 1890s, the Tan Hill drift mine still employed a dozen workers and there must have been a lively settlement to support them. The hidden shafts are now a hazard to travellers.

Apart from boasting a busy little mine, Tan Hill was a crossroads for cattle droves and packhorse trails. With so many hard-living, hard-drinking men about it is hardly surprising that someone opened an inn here. Any adjacent settlement has long gone, along with the drovers and jaggers, but the inn has survived and is now famous for its desolate location. It sits on a lonely road between Brough and Richmond, in an area of strange-sounding places like Moudy Mea and Arkengarthdale. The most exciting annual event is the Sheep Show (Swaledale sheep, naturally). Tan Hill Inn prides itself on being the highest pub in England (at 528m) but it also enjoys the worst weather, and makes this a virtue by promising

Pebble prominent moth.

snow, gales and freezing fog to anyone seeking a warm welcome and a log fire. The building is far from romantic (indeed, it is far from anything), but it offers first-rate accommodation and the beer is excellent.

One final test awaits walkers heading to the Stainmore Gap. This is Sleightholme

Moor, one of the nastiest wastes along the Way, still treacherous after more than forty years. People rarely get lost following the Frumming Beck to Trough Heads but they often get very wet. Like all the most notorious stretches, Sleightholme is usually saved for the fag end of a rainy day, when the views north to the Durham Dales are hidden behind a heavy veil. It is a place where the sun rarely seems to shine, and perhaps it is no coincidence that it is one of the best winter localities in the area for snow buntings, a bird usually at home in the arctic.

Blanket bog is in short supply in Europe; it is an endangered habitat and Britain accounts for far more than its fair share. Most of the peat formation, the deposition of undecayed *Sphagnum* moss in waterlogged conditions, started about five or six thousand years ago, when the climate turned wet and rich tundra soils were leeched of their nutrients and minerals. Britain's 'Atlantic' period (the 'climatic optimum', warm and humid) lasted long enough to cover most of the land with trees, but the combination of another climate change and the accumulation of

Bowes Castle in County Durham. The colossal walls were intended to repel Scottish attacks, but over the years they have also proved to be a useful free source of facing stone for local farms and houses.

a metre-thick layer of acid peat, plus the efforts of Neolithic farmers, gradually turned the uplands into barren heath, scrub and bog. In the Pennines these vast expanses were left to nature, and over the last century they have become our idea of 'wilderness': England's own Great Outdoors. Atmospheric pollution and recent agricultural practices (such as digging drainage channels or 'grips') have damaged many of the Pennine bogs; Sleightholme is a prime example of a degraded moor. Sometimes, it is possible to find boughs of birch and pine sticking out of peat hags as silent witness to the glory of the wild wood: paradise lost. There are also

A small wooden plaque commemorates the private school used by Dickens as the location for Dotheboys Hall in Nicholas Nickleby.

places where emerald carpets of *Sphagnum* still decorate the sikes and mires and are a reminder of what pristine peatlands were once like. But for most people, most of the time, Sleightholme is a dreary waste.

Stainmore is the halfway point of the Pennine Way. The A66 trans-Pennine trunk road can be crossed by heading directly north, or by turning north-east to overnight at the village of Bowes. The direct route is via God's Bridge, where the River Greta disappears underground at a limestone shelf or arch. Bowes is reached by following the river and crossing a footbridge near Lady Myers Farm. The path then passes the ruins of Bowes Castle, a great square Norman keep squatting over the site of a Roman fort. Archaeology confirms the importance of the Stainmore Gap as a natural crossing point for armies and for trade. It once marked the boundary between England and Scotland, and it was where the Norse King of Northumbria, Eric Bloodaxe, met an untimely end.

The village of Bowes hardly hints at the carnage it witnessed in the Border Wars. It is a taciturn place, reflecting grey clouds in grey stonework. One of its buildings is the original Dotheboys Hall, featured by Charles Dickens in 'Nicholas Nickleby'. Dickens often disguised fact within his fiction and there is no doubt that the publication of his story led to a public outcry and closure of the institution, one of the infamous 'Yorkshire Schools', where parents sent unwanted children in the 1830s. Many of the characters in the book were familiar figures in Bowes, including the dreadful headmaster Wackford Squeers and the poor simpleton, Smike. The real-life story had a satisfactory outcome: the evil headmaster was ruined and became a lonely cripple, whilst Smike (Edward Smith) ran away and was adopted by the village of Woodland, where he was a farmhand and sang at village functions. He died, a local hero, in 1884.

Redshank

Bowes to Forest-in-Teesdale

There seems to be a face and a clenched fist here at Goldsborough, which adds to the menacing atmosphere of the place.

Landscapes may be glorious or gloomy, dramatic or dull. Sometimes it is hard to define why a particular place evokes a particular emotion or impression. Cotherstone Moor, north of the A66 and the village of Bowes, is simply strange. For anyone who has spent the night at Bowes, the track back up onto the Pennine Way leads through wet pastures and deserted army ranges, where rusty signs still warn of poison gas. Then the route descends to a marshy hollow called Deep Dale and past a lonely steading called Levy Pool. There is something odd about Levy Pool. For decades, when the army were using the area for artillery practice, the farmhouse and outbuildings were left empty and derelict. Their roofs of pine purlins and heather thatch had rotted and collapsed. The stonework was crumbling. Then in the 1990s the ruin was bought and renovated, the gable end rebuilt and the farmhouse roof rethatched. But despite the efforts to preserve the 'black-thack' and bring Levy Pool back to life, the place still has a melancholy air about it, as if it has lived beyond its years.

The moors north of Levy Pool are wet and rushy: there is no heather for several miles. Some of the isolated rocks along the way bear prehistoric cup and ring marks incised into the millstone grit, perhaps as totems or waymarks. Similar or more elaborate cup and ring marks occur on the Yorkshire and Northumberland moors. Many still await discovery because they have been covered over by peat or vegetation. Perhaps the whole landscape was signed and decorated, but it is clear at least that most of the markings were close to trackways. So here on Cotherstone Moor the Pennine Way is only the latest long-distance path to trace a line north. There were and will be others.

The most prominent feature of Cotherstone Moor, visible from many miles around, is the flat-topped outcrop called Goldsborough. It looks as if it belongs in the Kalahari or in Utah: a place to attract the attention of bushmen and Anasazi hunter-gatherers. In fact archaeologists are now convinced that prominent or unusually shaped hills like this served as special or spiritual places in the Stone and Bronze Ages. The tribes of the Pennines must once have lived like the Kalahari bushmen, which is perhaps why they have left so few traces to be picked over. There have been archaeological finds at Goldsborough to indicate there were shelters below the rock faces, but it hardly needs scientific excavation to know that this must have been a 'sacred mountain'.

The 'Bowes Loop' or detour of the Pennine Way links up with the proper

Blood-drop emlets, a naturalised plant of streams and marshes, in a rushy hollow near Blackton Reservoir. Goldsborough is on the far skyline to the left of the farm.

route as it descends into Baldersdale, into a countryside of hayfields and improved pasture rather than grass/rush moorland. This is a place of reservoirs too; the River Balder was first dammed in 1894 to create Hury Reservoir, then Blackton Reservoir in 1896, and the larger Balderhead Reservoir was completed in 1965. Nearby, the Lune was dammed in 1915 to create Grassholme Reservoir, with Selset following in 1960. Although they clearly look artificial, these reservoirs fit into the landscape surprisingly well.

After the open moors of Cotherstone it comes as a surprise to find yourself in fields again as you cross the Balder. Farms and barns crowd the valley; the route passes Hagworm Hall ('hagworm' means adder)

Still waters at Baldershead Reservoir.

topped by wind-sculpted pines. It has an otherworldly feel to it and local legends associate it with ghosts and murders. Again, it is the site of a Bronze Age burial and again it is visible for miles around. It seems certain that the families who worked in the valley fields three thousand years ago wanted to be under the protection of their ancestors: they wanted to be able to look up to the most imposing skyline feature and feel in touch with both a spiritual and physical landscape. In those days the climate was warmer than it is today. Crops could be grown on the hillsides, but Bronze Age communities liked a prominent part of their settlement to be left alone, perhaps as a place for peace or contemplation. Rather like a churchyard, but dedicated to Nature rather than to God.

After the descent from Harter Fell the route of the Pennine Way turns west just before entering Middleton-in-Teesdale. People often miss Middleton out on their walk, preferring to overnight at Langdon Beck. This is a pity, partly because it is an interesting and colourful little town, and partly because there are some very acceptable cafes and pubs. The settlement

and Blackton Youth Hostel before climbing again, past Birk Hatt which was the home of the unlikely television celebrity, Hannah Hauxwell. The TV programmes made about Hannah in the 1980s portrayed her as living in a wild and remote dale, enduring a primitive and simple way of life. The latter was partly true, the former clearly not so; Baldersdale and Lunedale were never wild,

except on local dance nights. Today many of the farmhouses are converted into attractive executive dwellings, and the meadows are preserved for their wildlife value.

Before the Pennine Way reaches Teesdale it must climb again, onto the shoulder of Crossthwaite Common, where it passes another place with obvious spiritual significance. This is Kirkcarrion, a knoll

Pines top the ancient burial site of Kirkcarrion, north of Middleton-in-Teesdale. This view is from the east, but the tumulus is impressive from any direction.

grew out of the lead-mining bonanza that gripped the Durham Dales in the late eighteenth century. Carboniferous limestone is the bedrock of the Dales: among the layers of shale, sandstone and coal there is a major outcrop called the Great Limestone, and within this there are rich mineral veins. In medieval times it was silver that attracted the attention of speculators, but lead ore, galena, became the big business of the nineteenth century. The London Lead Company (known as the Quaker Company) established its headquarters here at Middleton and built an infrastructure of chapel, school, library and meeting room: enough to establish a proper community. Lead-mining was a flash in the pan; prosperity came and went in three or four generations, but the community endured.

Teesdale is a lovely part of the country. The walk along the sparkling river is a Pennine Way highlight, made extra special in June when the air is full of birdsong. In the meadows there are yellow wagtails and redshanks, on the rocks there are ring ouzels and wheatears, and in the riverside alders there are wood warblers and tree pipits. However, in several places along the dale it is clear that extractive industries have been at work and have left scars. There are some big quarries still working in the dale, providing local employment as well as dust and noise. The rock being extracted is dolerite, a fine-grained and very hard volcanic material, dark grey in colour and similar to basalt. It occurs as a ridge known as the Whin Sill, outcropping here in Teesdale and again at Hadrian's Wall and on the Northumberland coast at the Farne Islands. The Whin Sill's dolerite was formed from magma extruded or forced up through Carboniferous sediments. Because it cooled quickly the dolerite is fine-grained and hard, which is

White water cascades over black dolerite at High Force in Teesdale. The shoulders of the great waterfall are flanked by juniper woodland, and its lower banks are lined with shrubby cinquefoil.

why it is suitable for roadstone. Where it came into close contact with the Great Limestone it cooked the softer rock, changing it into more granular material which is known locally as sugar limestone. It is this hardened limestone, forming low outcrops above the main Whin Sill, that provides a unique habitat for some of Teesdale's famous rare flowers, such as spring gentian and Teesdale violet.

The varying hardness and softness of rocks makes a difference to the look of a landscape. They may feel equally solid to us, but beneath a glacier, sandstone outcrops behave like butter, dolerite like cheese: they will both erode, but at very different rates. When a river runs downhill over soft rock the flowing water gradually wears away a channel, helped by freezing and thawing. If the channel meets a harder floor of rock it takes longer to wear it away, creating a shelf. A waterfall is born. The Tees is notable for several waterfalls, especially High Force which has a cascade of nearly seventy feet, over a thick shelf of dolerite and a band of shale. Nearby is Low Force, more of a tumbling torrent, which is accessible from Bowlees car park via an old miners' bridge and is therefore a popular picnic spot. The whole stretch of river, from Wynch Bridge to Forest-in-Teesdale, is a lost world of botanic treasures: drifts of bird's eye primrose and alpine cinquefoil, and curious dwarf forests of juniper: relics from post-glacial Britain.

Sheep have scratched themselves against these relict juniper bushes for centuries, and it shows. In the distance is Cronkley Fell, one of the most famous botanic sites within the Teesdale National Nature Reserve.

Forest-in-Teesdale to Dufton

Teesdale at dawn, looking east from the head of the valley.

Upper Teesdale always looks a picture of pretty meadows and whitewashed farmhouses, the more verdant because the surrounding fells often loom dark and gloomy. The North Pennines has a character all its own, a wildness tempered by mining, quarrying, forestry and farming. At the last, it is the wildness that has prevailed.

The approach to land management of the high dales has changed over recent years, mainly because there is no profit in any of the traditional land uses. Agriculture survived here through government support, and the CAP (belatedly) has moved on.

The emphasis now is on conservation and access. Thus money finds its way to estate owners via English Nature, and tenants are encouraged to work with the elements, to touch the land lightly, by grazing fewer sheep and making hay rather than silage.

Most of Teesdale is owned by the Raby estate. The patchwork of small farms is a reminder of the days when the Durham Dales were studded with lead mines and quarries. To make ends meet, tenants worked the land in their 'spare time' whilst putting in a full week's labour in the extractive industries. Lead miners often stayed in bunkhouses (called 'shops') close to the mines, and only returned to

In the past, the cascade of Cauldron Snout would have varied with the latest storm. Now it is regulated as an outflow for Cow Green Reservoir.

their valley homes at weekends. It goes without saying that it was a hard life, but unlike in the North East coal mining industry, owners prided themselves on supporting their workers by providing schools, libraries and temperance clubs. Thus, a miner fought and drank through the week then went home to grow potatoes and take his wife to chapel.

The Pennine Way follows old miners' paths uphill from the Tees through meadows and pastures to the fells. Wynch Bridge, a little suspension footbridge at Bowlees, was built in 1830 to replace a previous ramshackle footbridge, which collapsed and killed a miner in 1820. On the fells, there are 'hushes' or trenches where water was dammed and then sent crashing down the slope, to expose mineral veins. Moss Shop, on the rise of Dufton Fell above Birkdale, is the site of a lead mine, but little remains to tell the tale except heather-covered spoil-heaps. In a landscape so influenced by industry, what you notice today is the way nature has brushed it all aside.

At Forest-in-Teesdale the Tees fragments and the Pennine Way follows the Harwood Beck before turning west over Widdybank

Hayfield and barn, Teesdale in County Durham.

Pasture. In early summer this is a place of arresting beauty, a patchwork of flowery meadows (hay rattle, eyebright, marsh orchid, meadow saxifrage). On the opposite bank of the shallow river is Cronkley: pasture even prettier, with banks of globeflower and wood cranesbill. In the old days (before the 1960s) hay was an essential crop on every farm. Meadows were grazed in early spring, then gated and left alone until July or early August, depending on the weather. Flowers grew

93

Lichen-covered blocks of dolerite line the Tees at Falcon Clints.

among the grass, and had time to flower and set seed before the cut. In recent decades grass yields have been increased by the use of new seed mixes sown as short-term leys, with applications of inorganic nitrogen fertilisers. A side-effect of this has been that slow-growing wild flowers have been unable to compete and have disappeared from meadows all over England. Worse still for the flowers, silage-making (cutting the grass in early summer and pickling it in black plastic bags) has superseded hay, because the crop is more reliable and does not need to be sun-dried.

It is only in the last few years, and in a very few places, that farmers have been encouraged by government grants to go back to a traditional hay-making system of organic fertilisers and a late cut. Teesdale is one of those places. Some grumpy old tenants had never quite seen the point of high input/high output farming in the first place, so some fields along the Pennine Way are as they have always been. Others are just starting to look

Wood cranesbill

94

High Cup from the Narrow Gate at Strands Beck, looking across to the east wall of High Cup Scar.

'natural' again as the fertilisers have been spared and the spring grass is no longer sappy and quick-growing. Of course, the spectacular effect of a change in meadow management is only visible to passers-by for a month or two each year. Even the best meadows are cropped and green when most Pennine Way walkers take to the hills.

Widdybank and Cronkley are both backed by famous fells, where rare mountain flowers thrive around outcrops of sugar limestone. Teesdale gained celebrity status in the 1960s when there was a public enquiry about the creation of a reservoir at Cow Green. The main argument in favour of the reservoir was that the industries of Teesmouth were expanding and would need more water, and that jobs would be created. Against this was the conservation interest, the potential damage to a unique ecosystem. Not surprisingly at that time, judgement went in favour of the reservoir. It is easy to say that the decision would have been different had the enquiry taken place today. Hindsight has proved that Cow Green was a white elephant and was never needed. But enquiries rarely have anything to do with justice or common sense and there are lots more white elephants waiting in the wings.

Having kept to pretty riversides for several miles the Pennine Way has to gain height to cross the great watershed of England, where East becomes West. At first the route is easy, climbing from Falcon Clints (a dolerite cliff face named after the peregrines that are always close by) up the boulder-banks of Cauldron Snout. At this point the tumbling river marks the county boundary, Durham into Cumbria. The famous waterfall has been tamed by Cow Green: the flow is controlled, so there are no droughts and no raging torrents. It always looks the same, always a picture-postcard,

Hay rattle

but just as contrived. A private road then leads west below the Cow Green dam to Birkdale, the last farm before the long climb to High Cup. Whatever time of year, and despite the recent addition of outbuildings, Birkdale marks the end of the civilised world and a step into frontier badlands.

Birkdale has only a few inbye fields; the rest is open fell and as marginal as agricultural land can ever be. It is marginal for walkers too, not because the landscape is anything less than inspiring, but because the underfoot conditions can be frightening. Until the last few years the slow pull up the valley of the Maize Beck was a nightmare, the miners' path often lost in cross-flows of black peat and bog-moss. Now the path is relatively dry and there are stone slabs across the worst of the runnels. Studying an OS map of this stretch of the Way is a fascinating business. Names like Stony Mea and Slegistone Band hint at a mining tradition, but thickly sprinkled all over Dufton and Murton Fells is the phrase 'shake holes', which sounds

worrying, and on the south side of the Maize Beck is a 'Danger Area', marked in red. In fact, shake holes are just circular depressions where underlying limestone has been dissolved by rainwater, and the Danger Area is an army training area, vaguely marked and rarely used by the army. There is no real hazard along the Pennine Way unless the weather turns against you, when everything is a hazard.

The feature that really grabs the attention on any map and in any description of the Pennine Way is High Cup, a deep wedge scooped out of the west face of the Cross Fell range. Nothing on paper is adequate to describe or prepare you for what is, simply, the most glorious landscape feature in northern England. You arrive at the pivotal point of High Cup Nick after having crossed High Cup Plain, the flat gathering-ground of Maize Beck. Suddenly you seem to be floating; the ground falls away and you are looking into an abyss with a tiny silver thread of a stream, High Cup Gill, far below you. On either side, arcing into the distance, are cliffs and pillars of dolerite, steely grey in sunlight or looming black out of the shadows. On most days there is a gusting wind funnelling up out of the valley, making you stoop and stagger. The views are breathtaking; this place is as spectacular as the Grand Canyon.

Having crossed the divide and contoured around the top edge of the Nick, along the Narrow Gate, you are facing the setting sun and the Lake District. It looks a different world and the descent into the Vale of Eden confirms the influence of a milder western climate. Dufton is a village of sandstone cottages glowing gold in evening sunlight, with shrub-filled gardens and flowering cherry trees. There is a Youth Hostel and a shop for provisions, a seat on the village green to sit and gather your thoughts, and a warm welcome at the Stag Inn.

Lunchtime at the Stag Inn in Dufton. The Eden Valley is more verdant and fertile than the Tees. After the austerity of the fells, the pub garden is a welcome distraction.

Half an hour after dawn on a still summer morning, looking south to Dufton Pike.

Dufton to Alston

Anticipation sometimes gives way to apprehension as walkers leave the homely village of Dufton and look to the summit of Cross Fell. It is the highest point along the Pennine chain and from the Eden valley it looks huge. Often, the plateau of the summit is capped by cloud; under certain weather conditions the warm air of the valley is sucked up to meet cold air, which creates first a cloud and then a searing wind, which howls back down into the valley. This 'Helm Wind' may have earned Cross Fell its original name, Fiends Fell. It is said to have been renamed after the seventh century missionary Paulinus held a service on the summit to convert the local heathens to the Roman church. Presumably a cross was erected to mark the spot and be visible to local settlements, but even after fourteen centuries it is difficult to imagine Cross Fell as anything but a pagan place.

The walk from Dufton follows a tree-lined lane, between pastures and from farm to farm, north by north-east and climbing steadily to open fell. At first, the dominant landscape features are the smooth green cones of Dufton Pike and Knock Pike; inliers which split away from the main Pennine

Footpath sign north of Dufton. In midsummer the verges are covered with cow parsley.

Great Dun Fell is topped by a radar installation, a surreal golf ball in the wilderness of the high fells. For people with just a day to explore the Cross Fell range there is an access road from Knock to Knock Ore Gill, a few hundred yards from the main ridge (but note that the installation and its approach road is off limits!).

Stone-slab footbridge over peaty ground on the climb to Cross Fell.

ridge many million years ago and became locked in softer sedimentary rock. Then the gradient quickens and for a mile or two there is no time to enjoy the scenery; the imperative is to climb. Eventually, somewhere near the currick or cairn of Knock Old Man, there is a chance to turn and look back over the Eden. Knock Pike is now in its proper perspective, far below. Ahead are the greatest links in the Pennine chain, Knock Fell, Great Dun Fell, Little Dun Fell and Cross Fell itself. This is a mighty landscape and the traverse along this ridge is an abiding memory for Pennine Way walkers. Sometimes the air is crystal-clear and the carpet of hard-rush, mat-grass, cloudberry and cotton grass shimmers emerald and ruby in cold morning sunshine. More often there is a mist or cloud or a piercing wind to mark the memories as a triumph of stamina over hostile elements.

It comes as something of a shock to realise that this remote and wild place is scarred by mine workings, especially by 'hushes' which are where gills or streams were dammed to create sufficient water to power-blast trenches and expose lead veins. Clearly, the paths we now use to explore the wilderness were made by miners. This was their workplace and they must have hated it. Another dent in the impression of wilderness is the Radar Station on the top of Great Dun Fell, this giant golf ball filters the heavens for civil aviation data and manages to look both silly and menacing. However, there is something magical about this landscape. What was once a dreadful boggy path north of Great Dun Fell is now stone-slabbed, so it is possible to look ahead rather than at your feet, and arrive at the deep

Wood tiger moth

Many derelict farmhouses and barns around the footings of Cross Fell have been renovated in the last few years, some are past redemption.

saddle before Cross Fell with a suitable sense of awe. Rainwater falling to your left is claimed by the Eden and flows west to the Solway; to the right it is claimed by the Tees and is coaxed east to the North Sea. This really is the Pennines' Great Divide.

What is clear straight away is that the summit of Cross Fell is quite different to its acolytes. It is broad and stony rather than boggy, dove-grey rather than dull green. After climbing the last steep pull, side-stepping boulders onto the rim of the

Alston on a Sunday morning. The little town is usually bursting with visitors looking for tea-shops and locals trying to park their 4x4s.

plateau and following cairn to cairn over the tabletop, you reach the wind-shelter and summit cairn at 893m (2,930 ft). This altitude may sound modest compared with the Alps, but latitude is important too: you are above the tree line and beyond any sort of comfort zone. The wind chill is fierce and there is no cover. The ground is shattered rock and glistening minerals, with a scatter of lichens and mosses. Anyone who has walked the near-tundra hilltops of Lapland will recognise just this kind of terrain,

Heron

and not be surprised that arctic birds like the dotterel and snow bunting turn up here from time to time. Orientation is straightforward if you can see the far hills; like Bleaklow and The Cheviot, Cross Fell can be a breezy stroll or a killer.

In these days of climate change, snowstorms come and go quickly on the Cumbrian fells. Falls are often fast and furious, then the wind sweeps the tops clear and fills in all the shake holes and gullies with a dazzling whiteness. Old snow may lie for weeks; in some years the north-east screes are covered until June, and there may be flurries and squalls of spindrift in August. Snow is dangerous because of what it hides. Anyone looking for a sublime single day's walk can do no better than choose a morning of deep frost when the ground is like iron and the air is still and dry. But walkers who have started out a week or more before cannot choose their weather for Cross Fell; they must take it as they find it and be careful where they put their feet on the long descent.

Whatever lies north of Cross Fell is likely to be an anticlimax, even if a third of the day still lies ahead. The landscape is lonely and handsome; the views from around Black Gut make the best photographs for a memento of the high fells. However, after the summit the long descent via the old Corpse Road to Garrigill, in the South Tyne valley, is easily forgotten. Travellers' tales often have gaps, and most Pennine Way walkers have half-days that they strain to recollect.

There are still signs of long-forgotten mines all along the slopes of the South Tyne valley. As the path descends along a walled track there may be a moment when you can imagine smoke and noise and the bustle of loading wagons. However, very little remains in situ. A few miles away over Flinty Fell, in the sister dales of the Nent and Upper Weardale, there are open air museums (Nenthead and Killhope) where it is possible to see the lead mining processes at work, to handle galena and walk along an adit or mineshaft. But on a long walk those experiences are for distant days, when you have the convenience of a car.

The South Tyne is another pretty river, shallow and stony like the Tees and the home of dippers and grey wagtails, herons and goosanders. However, there is a significant difference in the vegetation of the river gravels and terraces. Because of all the lead-mining, the ground is still polluted by heavy metals such as zinc and cadmium. Most common flowers fail to thrive in such conditions, and it is left to a small group of 'metallophytes' to colonise the open ground. Spring sandwort and alpine penny-cress, small and white, are the commonest metal-tolerant species, but there are places where thrift and kidney vetch thrive, and on the grassy river levels, drifts of mountain pansy make a fine show. Mountain pansy comes in several colour forms. On the high pastures it can be lemon-yellow, whilst here it is usually a velvety purple, sometimes so deep and rich in colour that it looks black and is therefore impossible to find in a field guide.

The gentle South Tyne walk leads the Pennine Way to Alston, a little market town resting at the confluence with the River Nent, which serves the trans-Pennine traffic from Hexham to Penrith. Alston used to be blessed with a sort of scruffy lead-mining chic and some curious shops. It still has a lot of character, but the steep cobbled main street and square is now a clutter of 4x4s and people-carriers. Lead-miners, foundry workers and farm labourers have been replaced by affluent middle-aged hippies with computer links. Alston survives on tourism, which has advantages if you are looking for comfortable accommodation and fine foods.

Alston in the chilly embrace of Cross Fell. A cold snap here can last two months.

Sunset from the Cross Fell range across the Eden Valley to the Solway.

Alston to Greenhead

Sometimes, on dark winter nights, Derwentwater's Lights appear across the northern sky. We now call them the Aurora and believe they are caused by solar activity, but in the eighteenth century they were associated with the death of James Radcliffe, third Earl of Derwentwater. Alston was one of his family's properties; they also owned land at Dilston Hall in Northumberland and in the Lake District near Keswick (hence the family title). James was an illegitimate son of Charles II and supported the Jacobite Rebellion of 1715, for which he paid with his head. The family properties were given to the Greenwich Hospital, who later leased the Alston mines to the London Lead Company.

Alston from the west bank of the South Tyne.

Suckler cattle outside the ramparts of the Roman fort at Whitley Castle.

Alston owes its quirky appearance to its sudden expansion in the early nineteenth century, when lead-mining brought a flurry of jobs to the area and there was a sudden demand for accommodation. Sturdy houses were built and existing terraces were separated into flats, with new doors and extra flights of stairs to the street. There was no plan, development just happened, and when the bonanza fizzled out (because of cheap foreign competition) the town stuttered and smouldered until the coming of the railways.

The Haltwhistle-Alston branch line served the South Tyne valley for over a century. It closed in 1976 but left a few reminders of its infrastructure, notably Lambley Viaduct which has been renovated and can now be crossed on foot for picturesque views of the South Tyne. A couple of miles of track north of Alston has been reopened as a narrow-gauge railway and allows tourists to go for picnics to Kirkhaugh.

The Pennine Way has to find a route north to Greenhead and the Tyne Gap. There is no dramatic way of doing this, so the path dithers on the shoulder of the South Tyne valley, rarely within sight of the river and never able to strike out over the moors. There are compensations for this enforced strategy. One particular side-step of the route takes you up via Wanwood Bent (a glorious name for a boggy pasture) to cross the Gilderdale Beck into Northumberland. A path then climbs to Whitley Castle, the site of an important Roman fort guarding the Maiden Way. No stones are left standing, but there are impressive earth banks and ditches. Roman soldiers must have marched up the South Tyne hoping their postings were not going to be as uncomfortable as they had heard back at their headquarters in York. They may have camped here before joining the legions manning the Stanegate in the Tyne valley, then headed north again beyond the edge of the Empire, where Calgacus had gathered his Caledonian army, 'the last of the free', in a gesture of defiance. It was all a long time ago, but in this windswept place history is often measured in a few inches of earth. The best sort of archaeology feeds off a fertile imagination.

Back downhill and across the A689 at the scruffy and badly signed Castle Nook, the character of the walk changes again and

Jack-by-the-hedge

leads through pretty buttercup meadows and old pastures via Kirkhaugh. There are two common species of buttercups here: bulbous buttercup and meadow buttercup, the former short and with sepals bent back beneath the petals, the latter tall and with sepals cupping the petals. In old rigg and furrow pastures the bulbous buttercup will be growing on the dry ridge-crests and the meadow buttercup in the damper hollows. All buttercups are poisonous to

A century ago bracken was relatively scarce , managed by farmers and cut for winter bedding. Now it has invaded whole landscapes but adds vibrant colour to the uplands. A Pennine Way stile north of the Glendue Burn.

Lambley Viaduct, a short detour east off Lambley Common on the South Tyne Trail in south Northumberland. The viaduct has recently been renovated and it is possible to walk across it for views of the river and the wooded valley.

stock; they also taste nasty so are avoided. Which is why some of the richest pastures are choked with buttercups. The South Tyne is never very far away, across a field or two to the east, but it is only for a few hundred yards at Thompson's Well that the path and river meet: the route follows the modern road, which in turn is on the line of the Roman road.

From Burnstones there are two ways to reach Lambley: by following the proper route which clips the edge of the Geltsdale moors, and by walking along the old railway line, which is now managed by Northumberland County Council. The disused railway line is a safe and gentle stroll, pretty in early summer when alders and sallows are into leaf. However, most people who have got this far on the Pennine Way are ready for the high ground again and the heather moors of Glendue and Geltsdale are particularly attractive, both in late summer when the heather is in flower and in early winter when there is a chance of seeing birds of prey. A big slice of these remote moors (i.e. about five thousand hectares) is owned by the RSPB, who manage it for wildlife and are trying to increase the breeding success

Some years are better than others, but the Northumbrian/Cumbrian moors always put on a good show of heather in August.

112

of birds like the black grouse and the hen harrier. Hen harriers at Geltsdale used to make the local news because they were shot or persecuted. Over the last few years there have been sporadic breeding successes, and there is a chance of seeing jevenile birds anywhere between here and Cow Green, but the future of the hen harrier in England is still in the balance.

In spring the tall heather on this side of the moor looks dark and dormant, but in fact this is the best time to notice some of the impressive insects that are associated with the habitat. Full-grown caterpillars of northern eggar and fox-moths often sit out in full view along the bare pathside. They are usually safe from birds - their fur is irritating and only cuckoos can swallow them. However, a large proportion are attacked by parasitic wasps, which lay their eggs into the caterpillars in the previous autumn. The larvae then develop inside their host until they are ready to pupate. Some of the big furry caterpillars that seem to be sunning themselves on the heather may in fact be feeling very unwell, as their uninvited guests are preparing to wriggle their way out.

The Pennine Way and South Tyne Trail meet at the Knar Burn viaduct, north of Slaggyford.

On sunny days bees and wasps, beetles, flies and moths are all very active on the moors. Heather is a rich source of nectar in late summer and showy species like the big Volucella hoverflies and the heath bumblebee make a real buzz as they go about their business. The noise, as well as the scent and the colour of heather moorland, can be intense and magical.

The path on the east shoulder of the moor keeps closely to the Maiden Way. In Roman times this wild area would have been the territory of the Brigantes, one of the most hostile of the British tribes. They were subdued but not quite tamed and it is quite likely that in the early days of pacification the legionaries had to watch their backs as they crossed hostile territory. In the end, Brigantian families probably succumbed to a taste of the good life rather than to defeat in battle. Consumer goods were the Romans' secret weapon. What exactly this landscape looked like two thousand years ago is a mystery but it was probably rough heathland or scrub. Heather would have been here, but not as an unbroken carpet. Seas of purple heather are a product of intense grouse management and only

Map-reading in the South Tyne Valley.

appeared in the nineteenth century as the wealth of the Industrial Revolution was translated into country estates. This area gained a living from coal mining and extractive industries still scar the landscape. To the north of Halton-lea-Gate are Hartleyburn and Blenkinsopp Common, overgrazed and sodden, which may more closely resemble the Brigantian wastes.

After remote and lonely moorland, the A69 comes as an ugly but welcome sight, usually reached late in the day when civilisation beckons. The prosaic little village of Greenhead, complete with a Youth Hostel, tearoom and a pub, is a regular Pennine Way stopover. Any black dog seen wandering the streets should be avoided: it may be the ghost from nearby Blenkinsopp Hall.

Greenhead to Steel Rigg

Mule lambs in the pasture east of Longbyre, looking towards Thirlwall Castle.

The Tyne Gap is one of Britain's natural divides, a verdant corridor between the Solway and Tynemouth. Greenhead lies at its pivot: to the west flow the Irthing and the Eden, to the east are the South Tyne and Tyne. To the north and south there are high hills and moors. Over the years it is hardly surprising that the isthmus has been of strategic as well as economic value. William the Conqueror and Edward I both came this way to hammer the Scots, or try to, and in the eighteenth century, a military road was laid between Carlisle and Newcastle, as a rapid-response measure to Jacobite insurgence. But, of course, the Tyne Gap is best known for being the northern frontier of the Roman Empire.

In the early days of conquest and pacification, Agricola cut a swathe through the Brigantian tribes of the North Pennines and built a series of forts across the narrow neck of country, linking these by a road known as the Stanegate. But Vespasian's great general never clinched a final victory in the far north, and the Caledonians were an increasing nuisance through the reign of Trajan. When a new Emperor, Hadrian, visited the province in AD122 he came up with a drastic solution: he instructed his governor, Aulus Platorius Nepos, to build a wall. The enterprise took about eight years

The ruins of Thirlwall Castle, a medieval tower-house on a knoll above the Tipalt Burn near Greenhead.
Stone for Thirlwall's thick skin was 'quarried' from nearby Hadrian's Wall.

and through its long and eventful working life the Wall came to represent both the power and the vulnerability of the Empire. Its main purpose was probably to deter barbarian tribes and to keep the legions gainfully employed. It was breached several times, and for long periods it served as little more than a customs barrier. When it was finally abandoned in the early fifth century it is arguable whether the Wall had been a military success, but it certainly made a mark in history and it is now one of the most famous ruins in Europe.

All of this raises a high level of expectation when you explore the landscape of the Wall country. To avoid disappointment it is important to realise how little of the monument has survived. It is also important to give your imagination time to work on boggy ditches and grassy knolls. For most of its seventy-three miles the Wall is missing, having been dismantled over the years for building stone. Most of the original facing stone, and an assortment of inscribed tablets and altarpieces, can be seen in local barns and farmhouses. However, some stretches of the Wall were too remote to be robbed, and these coincide with the

Less than half its original height, but still an unmissable object. Hadrian probably intended the Wall as a deterrent and a clear demarcation of the limits to his Empire.

One of the best, most intact, sections of Hadrian's Wall, near Walltown. The Pennine Way and Hadrian's Wall Nation Trails coincide for a few miles to follow the Whin Sill.

Lesser celandine

most dramatic countryside. In particular, the Romans made full use of natural land forms. They let rivers and marshes, hill-crests and cliffs augment their defences. The most daunting and glorious stretch of the Wall runs along the Whin Sill, the same geological feature responsible for Falcon Clints and High Cup in Teesdale. Here in Northumberland, the dolerite ridge runs east-west and has a gentle south slope and a steep or vertical north face. Wherever possible, and for as long as the sill outcrops, the Romans followed the crest of the ridge. The completed Wall defences included a V-shaped ditch on the north side, a sequence of ditches and banks, called the Vallum, a few yards away to the south, and a Military Way for access. Every Roman mile (which measured a little less then a modern mile) there was a milecastle and a pair of turrets, and the whole system was supported by a network of forts, either specially built or adapted from the Stanegate system. It was a colossal undertaking and, with minor modifications, it served its purpose for nearly three hundred years.

The Pennine Way joins the line of the Wall a few hundred yards north of Greenhead,

Great Chesters and the site of Aesica Roman Fort. The line of Hadrian's Wall (without any stonework on this stretch) climbs from Caw Gap to the fort, then up to the crest of the Whin Sill.

at a place called Thirlwall. The name is significant, because 'thirl' means to cast down: it was probably here that the Romans suffered a shattering defeat in the 'Barbarian Conspiracy' of 367. The absence of the Wall today is nothing to do with the Picts or Scots: the stonework was gathered up in the fourteenth century and used for the building of a great tower house called Thirlwall Castle. Its imposing ruins occupy a hilltop or motte on a bend of the River Tipalt: the site is accessible and is worth a close look.

East of Thirlwall the Way follows the obvious Wall ditch, past the unexcavated site of Carvoran Roman Fort (close to the Roman Army Museum) and through the landscaped workings of Walltown Quarry, where dolerite ('whinstone') was extracted until the 1970s, for use as paving setts, cobbles and roadstone. To see a big piece of the Whin Sill cut away comes as a shock, but as at the smaller quarry at Cawfields, at least this allows you to appreciate the geology of the volcanic intrusion and how the dolerite has cooled like basalt into rough hexagons and columns. Both quarries are now picnic sites.

Beyond Walltown Quarry the Way climbs onto the ridge again and meets a proper section of the Wall for the first time. It is a dramatic moment, in a dramatic setting. For the next few miles the Wall soars and swoops, always clinging to the crest of the ridge. In places it stands six or seven feet high (its original height was probably fifteen feet) and most of the turrets and milecastles are visible, at least as foundations. Running parallel to the south is the

Vallum; the area in between was the military zone. At Great Chesters the Way passes through a Roman fort (Aesica), complete with the weathered remains of a vaulted strongroom and an altar. At Windshields the Way climbs to the highest point on the Whin Sill; if the weather is kind the views are panoramic, with Cross Fell to the south and the Solway Firth to the west. But the chances are that one or both of these will be shrouded in mist or cloud.

Walking the Wall is surprisingly tiring, even if you are fit. This is because the path has to lose and regain height all the time as it crosses gaps in the ridge. In the Ice Age this entire landscape was buried under a glacier, which creaked and gauged its way eastwards, scouring the softer sedimentary rock and plucking away anything detachable. Erosion was not so severe for the hard dolerite; the ridge survived intact, but beneath the massive weight of ice, pressurised water forced its way through the solid rock, creating what are called

The highest point (345m) of Hadrian's Wall, on Windshields Crags, north-east of Haltwhistle. The line of the Wall is represented here by an ordinary drystone wall.

Early morning east of Windshields looking towards Peel Crags, Crag Lough and Hotbank.

meltwater channels. These are the steep-sided 'nicks' that characterise the Whin Sill today.

In 1801, when nobody bothered very much about 'antiquities', an old man called William Hutton walked all the way from his home in Birmingham to explore the Wall. It was his life's great adventure. 'Perhaps,' he wrote in his diary, 'I am the first man that ever travelled the whole length of this Wall, and probably the last that ever will attempt it... Old men are much inclined to accuse youth of their follies; but on this head silence will become me, lest I should be asked, "What can exceed the folly of that man, who, at seventy-eight, walked six hundred miles to see a shattered Wall!"'

Hutton encountered the same sort of problems in finding accommodation as Pennine Way walkers do today: 'A more dreary country than this ...can scarcely be conceived... As the evening was approaching, and nature called loudly for support and rest ...I was obliged to retreat to the military road, to the only public house ...known by no other name than that of Twice Brewed.'

But, at first, Hutton was out of luck. 'You must be so kind as to indulge me with a bed,' he said. 'I will be satisfied with anything.' 'I cannot, except that you will sleep with this man,' said the landlady, pointing to a poor sick traveller. 'That will be inconvenient,' said Hutton. However, the only other option was to agree to share a bed with a young boy. 'Having completed our bargain, and supped, fifteen carriers approached, each with a one-horse coach, and sat down to pudding and beef, which I soon perceived were not too large... The tankard too, like a bowl lading water out of the well, was oft emptied, oft filled. My landlady, however, swerved from her agreement; for she found me a whole bed to my wish.'

Adventures are an essential ingredient of long-distance walking. When Hutton hit the trail again next morning it was with a lighter step. 'Becoming a gainer at Twice Brewed by a broken promise, which is seldom the case, I retreated...over a Moss to my favourite pursuit, which brought me to House-Steads... Here lie the remains of antient splendour.'

The Twice Brewed is still in business, next door to the Once Brewed Youth Hostel and National Park Visitor Centre.

Hutton would have been astonished at the number of people who now visit the Wall, and would have been gratified that he had helped to prevent some sections from being plundered by local builders. According to his daughter he walked the whole six hundred miles in one pair of shoes 'and scarcely made a hole in his stockings'.

The north-facing cliff of the Whin Sill, near Steel Rigg. Cracks and fissures in the grey dolerite columns provide a roothold for rowan, downy birch, aspen and hawthorn.

Steel Rigg to Bellingham

Red campion

Hadrian's Wall and the Whin Sill coincide for just a few miles in south Northumberland, creating a hotspot in a cold county. Thousands of visitors who only have an hour or two to spare converge on the dramatic but accessible section between the car park at Steel Rigg and Housesteads Fort. Anyone walking the National Trail and hitting this central section at a weekend might feel cheated of solitude but at least the crowds are gathered in one place and are soon left behind: the Pennine Way turns north before it reaches Housesteads.

Steel Rigg is deceptive. Close to the car park there is a level section of Wall and a flattish sweep of pasture, where the Roman Wall Show is held every summer. A few steps further east the crest of the ridge dips and then rises sharply again: the going is never easy. However, unlike many of the nicks in the ridge, Peel Gap lets you wander around to the steep north face of the Whin Sill, to have a look at the grey columns of dolerite and the tumbled boulders that are the home of alpine plants like parsley fern and clubmoss. There is a cathedral calm about this place. It is, of course, on the barbarian side of the frontier.

The Wall is in good shape all the way to Housesteads. Most of the stonework has been consolidated and some sections have been rebuilt (a century ago: no one would dare to do so today), but there is still a feeling of ruinous antiquity about Castle Nick and Sycamore Gap, where the path skips over the footings from one side of the

Castle Nick, with the shell of Milecastle 39 and its internal lay-out of rooms and stables marked out by stone footings.

Crag Lough and Hotbank Farm, from the crest of the Whin Sill.

Wall to the other. Milecastle 39, with Crag Lough in the distance, is a familiar sight even for those who have never set foot in the area before; it appears in hundreds of calendars and brochures, as does the view of Cuddy's Crags to the east.

Apart from the obvious Roman stones and earthworks on the slope of the Whin Sill there are a few places where more modest remains, often no more than hummocks in the shallow turf, mark the site of medieval shielings, where local farmers or their families came each summer to graze their cattle. Long after the Roman Empire was forgotten, and for hundreds of years until the eighteenth century, this land was bandit country and a wasteland. Nobody dared to live here permanently. Border conflicts between proud kings north and south of the border degenerated into feuds and murderous cattle raids; the authorities created a buffer zone where Marcher Lords meted out rough justice but neighbour preyed upon neighbour. Reiving became a way of life and local families like the Armstrongs gained notoriety and a transient wealth, which sometimes only lasted until the next revenge raid. The sweep

Ridley Common where the Pennine Way strikes north from the Wall at Rapishaw Gap.

of country north of the Wall has a bleakness about it that speaks of hard times. When agricultural innovation was transforming the countryside to the south, no landowner would invest in this boggy waste.

Crossing the stile at Rapishaw Gap and heading out from the Wall brings you into a wide landscape of rolling pastures, often washed pink and sienna by bleached moor-grass and hard-rush. The bedrock is sedimentary sandstone and shale, in rolling waves and with occasional outcrops of muddy limestone and coal. During the last Ice Age a vast glacier ran west to east,

128

chiselling and flattening the soft rocks. When the ice melted around 12,000 years ago, it left behind a tundra plain of shallow lakes, which gradually choked themselves in rafts of bog-moss and carr-woodland. A few lakes have survived into modern times, and they have an impact on the scenery out of all proportion with their size. They have also proved to be of interest to archaeologists; cores of mud extracted from bogs and lake-beds have produced pollen profiles, demonstrating how extensive cereal farming was during Roman times (the Wall garrison comprised about 30,000 hungry men), and how woodland

Brooklime

Thick walls and small windows were a prudent defence for farmers with anything worth stealing in the Border Wars. In more peaceful times, after the Union of the Crowns, many of the 'bastle' houses were left to decay. Others were adapted as barns or outhouses, as here at Lowsteads.

The Warks Burn, east of Stonehaugh. Pretty peat-stained burns are a feature of the rolling pastures and plantations north of the Wall. Fragments of oak woodland along the burn are the home of redstart and wood warbler.

Milkwort

regeneration soon followed when the frontier was abandoned in the early fifth century.

Crag Lough sits at the foot of the dolerite cliff of Highshield Crags and creates a dizzying blue mirror as you look down from the cliff-top path beside the Wall. A mile out to the north and east are Greenlee and Broomlee Loughs; the Pennine Way seeks out the dry ground between them, probably following a long-forgotten reivers' trail. On a still winter's morning you are likely to see whooper swans flighting overhead from one lough to the other, or hear their stirring calls far in the distance. Sometimes there are greylag geese here too, and perhaps a peregrine or a hen harrier. This remote place is their world: you are passing through.

Most of the open land north of the Whin Sill, made infamous in the Border Wars, is now either improved pasture or spruce plantation. Wark Forest is dull, even allowing for recent improvements by Forest Enterprise, who are trying to reverse previous follies by block-felling some sections of their vast Border Forest, by planting more broadleaf trees and by damming drains. Surviving bogs (collectively known as the Border Mires) are now considered to be of international importance for wildlife. It is an irony that society suddenly values wilderness more than it needs wood pulp. Many of the mires which are transformed each June from smelly peat-flows to a living carpet of flowers (bog rosemary, cranberry, cotton grass etc.) exist as tiny clearings in the forest. Here and there, the Pennine Way flirts with them, sufficient to appreciate their treacherous beauty before pressing on over Haughton Common.

The Warks Burn is a miniature white-water torrent, nestling in a rocky cleft and half-hidden by trees. Tall oaks harbour more

Step-stile south of Horneystead above the valley of the Warks Burn.

than their share of northern songbirds (wood warbler, redstart, pied flycatcher), but once these pretty migrants have found a nest-site and sung their way into family life they fall silent and are impossible to locate in the foliage. On a brief visit you will see lots of chaffinches but not much else.

Serious walking allows you to appreciate wildlife habitats but not to encounter special or characteristic species, which may be secretive or seasonal. This principle certainly applies to the major river of the area, the North Tyne, which the Way crosses on its approach to the market town of Bellingham. The North Tyne is one of the best otter rivers in the country, but few people ever catch a glimpse of a wild otter: they are creatures of the twilight.

The countryside north of Warks Burn is pastoral rather than dramatic. It has been good farmland for centuries and there is no reason to doubt that it was cultivated in Roman times. In the dark days of the Border Wars, rural communities were vulnerable and were often attacked, either by foraging troops or by reivers.

Clearly, farmers were an easy and popular target, and cattle were a valuable asset. Having been put to the torch once too often, farming families in the border zone adopted a pragmatic lifestyle and a dour vernacular architecture. Their homes were built with walls four feet thick and with massive barred oak doors. Downstairs these 'bastle-houses' had no windows and no stairs. In times of danger a family could gather its grain and best stock into the lower room and climb a ladder into the small upper room. The ladder was then pulled up and the trapdoor locked. Then the family waited to be rescued. Border ballads relate many blood-curdling tales of what it was like to be on the receiving end of a raid. Not every family survived the ordeal: some were smoked out and murdered.

Because they were so sturdily built, many bastle-houses have survived for over four hundred years and can be seen today, sometimes as ruins but often as barns or farm outbuildings. The Pennine Way passes at least two on its way through the pasturelands of the Blacka Burn, at Horneysteads and at Lowsteads.

The pepperpot or bell shaped monument on the summit of Padon Hill. A panoramic view over the Dargues Burn to Otterburn.

Brown hare

Bellingham to Byrness

There are very few settlements between Tynedale and Redesdale, which is why the little market town of Bellingham (pronounced Bellinjum) is a welcome stopover for Pennine Way walkers. At first sight it is not the prettiest of places to spend an evening. Tomlinson's 'Comprehensive Guide to Northumberland', published in 1888, described it as 'dull and uninviting', explaining that it had not yet recovered from the border troubles when 'the less attractive a town was the fewer temptations it offered to the lawless inhabitants of the Borderland'. Bearing this in mind, Bellingham has fared well in the face of adversity: any grey austerity is compensated for these days by the cheerful shops and pubs, and by a well-placed Youth Hostel.

After crossing the road bridge into the town from the south, the Pennine Way follows the riverside and climbs a path uphill beside the parish church of St Cuthbert's. The path is pretty and usually flanked by flowers. A spring, known locally as Cuddy's Well, adds an extra touch of magic to the spot. Cuthbert, Bishop of Lindisfarne in the glory days of the seventh century, is the North-East's favourite saint and his name (or its diminutive, Cuddy) appears attached to all sorts of places. The church is unusual because it has a stone-slabbed roof - a response to Scottish raids when the original wooden roof was torched at least twice. In the little graveyard is an unusual gravestone shaped like a woolpack. Legend has it that it is a robber's grave, but

the town was once host to the biggest wool fair in the region and the grave is probably an indication of a trade or occupation. Bellingham recently lost its market (in the wake of the foot-and-mouth outbreak of 2001), but there is still a lively shepherds' show in late August.

Just out of Bellingham to the north is one of Northumberland's prettiest wooded denes, with a waterfall at its head called Hareshaw Linn. Unfortunately there is no path out of the dene and so the Pennine Way has to detour around it to reach the open moorland, via old iron workings and drift mines to Callerhues Crags and Hareshaw Head. This expanse of moorland is wide and limitless, the colour and texture of rich brocade and

Spruce logs awaiting collection, beside a block of clear fell in Kielder Forest, on the path down to Blakehopeburnhaugh. Most of the smaller wood goes for chipboard.

like these, that the spirit of the Pennine Way reasserts itself: it asks serious questions.

In a country of few landmarks, the pepperpot cairn on Padon Hill is unmistakable. It stands atop the highest point in a chain of hills that includes Deer Play, Whitley Pike and Brownrigg Head: all have panoramic views, west over boggy moorland to the upper North Tyne Valley, east over boggy moorland to Redesdale. The cairn on Padon Hill is a recent creation, placed there in the 1920s by the then owners of Otterburn Hall, the Morrison-Bells, who liked the idea of being able to see a bell-shaped monument from their mansion. However, there was a cairn of some sort on Padon Hill long before the Bells arrived. In fact there was probably a huge pile of stones here in the Bronze Age, marking a burial and acting as a tribal gathering place. Much later, in the seventeenth century, local people climbed Padon Hill to hear the sermons of a Presbyterian minister called Alexander Peden. In those dark days of religious persecution, God was often worshipped at 'conventicles' in the open, in secret and from a good vantage

the essence of Northumberland, with windswept moor-grass and heather and virtually no trees. This can be unpredictable country: snow squalls can arrive on the back of a summer breeze, and a day that started brightly can end with walkers trying to find an escape route in thick mist. Footpaths may be five miles from any settlement, and even further from a B & B. Paths may not be waymarked: mobile phones may not work. It is at times like this, and in places point. The congregation each carried a stone with them to add to the cairn, so that their defiance could be seen from afar, for those who knew how and where to look. Alexander Peden led a fugitive existence, sleeping in caves and travelling by forgotten ways. He died in 1686, one step ahead of the King's dragoons.

One of the big changes in the English uplands over the past fifty years, and therefore within the working life of the Pennine Way, has been the increase in forestry. Many conifer plantations appeared after the Great War as a response to a perceived shortage of timber, for pit props etc. The Forestry Commission was created with a simple remit, to grow trees: to buy land and plant it with quick-growing conifers. There was never any question of an amenity or conservation role for the new forests: that came very much later. Sitka and Norway spruce, lodgepole pine and larch were planted across swathes of Northumberland in the 1950s and '60s. Big expanses of land could be bought cheaply from near-feudal estates. Shepherds were put out of their homes and any wildlife habitats or

The longest place name in England: Cottonshopeburnfoot.

archaeological sites were planted over as if they did not exist. And in time they did not. In the 1970s and '80s, private forestry firms, backed by government grants or tax incentives, continued the process by filling in gaps and leasing land that should never have been planted. In the end, a fifth of Northumberland National Park was under forest, and a separate Kielder Forest had been created, stretching from Kershope and Spadeadam all the way to Catcleugh at the head of Redesdale.

There is a point on the descent from Padon Hill when the dark green ribbon beyond the moors resolves itself into trees, and at Brownrigg Head the Pennine Way turns north-west and enters Kielder Forest. This moment brings a chill to the heart of most walkers. The prospect of being enclosed, of seeing little sky and no horizon for several miles, is greeted like a prison sentence. Fortunately the terrain is easy and the claustrophobia is soon over. Also, there is a good chance of seeing roe deer, red squirrels, crossbills and goshawks, the small band of creatures that have benefited from forestry. There is a silence and a spirit in the conifer plantations too, quite different to the exhilaration of wide open spaces and different again to the timeless calm of oak woodland. In fact, there is a feeling of transience about spruce forests. For a few years they are fresh and green, then shadowy and grey, and then they are swept away by a Locomo Harvester, dispatching four hundred tonnes of timber a week. Most of the wood is of poor quality and is sent to be made into chipboard, newsprint, pallets and cardboard. The clear-felled coupes that are left behind

Out from the forest: the approach to Byrness from Blakehopeburnhaugh, in Redesdale.

resemble battlefields; mud wallows and peat ridges with splintered branches and severed stumps exposed to cold sunlight.

Down into Redesdale the forest rides are flanked by birch, rowan and oak and there is a less formal arrangement to the plantings, all part of Forest Enterprise's plan to attract visitors and be recognised as a proper conservation agency. As it approaches the Rede the path meets green pastures in a

Holy Trinity Church, Byrness, above the River Rede. Byrness is the last settlement south of the Border at Carter Bar.

is called Blakehopeburnhaugh. The name is simply descriptive: 'blake' means black, a 'hope' is a side-valley, a 'haugh' is a strip of pasture along a valley, and a burn is a stream. A little further up Redesdale is Cottonshopeburnfoot i.e. the place where the Cottonshope Burn meets the Rede. These are the longest official place-names in England. They may not be as long as certain Welsh place names, but clearly they have been generated in just the same prosaic way.

The last mile of the Way to Byrness is an easy meander beside the river pastures, leading to the tiny church of Holy Trinity. Inside is a beautiful stained glass window, commemorating the work of the navvies who built nearby Catcleugh Reservoir. Walkers without transport have the option here of camping at Cottonshopeburnfoot, or staying at either Byrness Youth Hostel or Byrness Hotel. What lies ahead is the Cheviot traverse, which needs to be undertaken after a good night's sleep.

narrow defile, still with the forest on either side. The Rede is a delightful little river. The river's name ('rede' = red) refers to the colour of its water, which is supposed to have run with blood after the Battle of Otterburn, but is more likely to have been so-named because of peat that stains it to the colour of a Strathspey malt.

The first little settlement upstream, not much more than a clearing in the forest,

Redesdale can be the coldest place in England. The Pennine Way climbs quickly out of the forest to Byrness Hill from where there are good views to Catcleugh Reservoir and the Border.

Byrness to Clennell Street

Most paths across the Cheviot Hills follow old drove roads used in the eighteenth century when great herds of cattle were driven from Scotland to markets in the south. These trackways or 'streets' seek out the easiest and grassiest ground, usually heading north-west/south-east. The Pennine Way follows a different trend, keeping wherever possible to the highest ground and the most spectacular scenery, along the border ridge. The going here is tough and the terrain sometimes boggy. It is twenty-five miles from Byrness in Redesdale to Kirk Yetholm in the Bowmont Valley; between these settlements there is no accommodation on the route, and no shelter except a couple of bleak refuge-huts. Walkers allowing themselves two days for the crossing have either to take a tent or detour down into Coquetdale to find a farmhouse.

Tom Stephenson, first advocate of the Pennine Way and the most famous outdoor writer of his day, knew the Cheviot landscape well: 'Looking over that great expanse... those great rounded hills and deep winding valleys and the play of light over them, I think probably I would plump for the Cheviots as my favourite ground.' By contrast, Wainwright, who wrote the first popular guide to the Pennine Way, likened the traverse on the last leg of the route to Scott's expedition to the South Pole, describing it as 'a long hard walk. Damned long. Damned hard. Especially in rain.' They were both right, of course.

The Cheviots can be glorious: Wainwright caught them on a bad day.

Most of the Cheviot massif is composed of volcanic rock: lava and ash piled up from a long-extinct volcano. Beneath the extensive covering of andesite, a core of magma was pushed up but did not reach the surface. It cooled slowly to form granite. When the mountain range was worn down by glaciers the granite was exposed, and because the igneous rock was hard, it eroded only slowly, creating what are now the 2,000-foot hills known as The Cheviot and Hedgehope. Immediately around the granite core, where the andesite had come into contact with the magma and been baked into a hard circlet or aureole, rock tors like pimples stand out on the smooth skin of the land. But most of the Cheviot Hills are andesite.

From Byrness village the Pennine Way climbs quickly through pine and spruce plantations to reach the open crest of Byrness Hill. Each hill then rises higher: Houx Hill, Ravens Knowe, Brownhart Law, Lamb Hill, Beefstand, Mozie Law and Windy Gyle. Fine names for grand steps along the way.

At first, Redesdale Forest crowds the foreground. The main plantations date back to the 1960s. At that time a lookout post stood on the brow of Byrness Hill, providing an overview of the young Border Forest. The building has gone but this is still an outstanding place to stop for a view of upper Redesdale. The forest is now thoroughly established and seems to stretch to the skyline; in fact, it stops short of the border at Carter Bar but extends far to the south-west, lapping around the remote moorlands of Deadwater, Emblehope and Kielderhead and swallowing up Wauchope and Kershope. Redesdale at least has the benefit of varied terrain. In the middle distance, looking west from Byrness Hill, is Catcleugh Reservoir, built in the 1900s

Ammophila hunting wasp

Acorn waymark on the ascent from Byrness.

High, wide and handsome hills on the Border Ridge near Brownhart Law. Dere Street, the Roman Road to the North, crosses the Cheviots by a direct route and this is where one of their signal stations was sited. In the far distance are the Eildon Hills - site of the Roman fort of Trimontium.

to supply industrial Tyneside. The navvies who worked on the construction lived in a purpose-built settlement of wooden huts, separated into two communities called Newcastle and Gateshead. After the navvies left, Byrness became a ghost town and most of the huts were demolished. Then came the Forestry Commission, who built a new village of brick terraced houses, intending them to be a permanent base for a large team of foresters. Mechanisation put paid to that idea, and most of the scattered workforce managing the forest is now contract labour.

Before Redesdale Forest the vegetation of the valley and lower hill slopes was dominated by purple moor-grass, creating pink prairies. In autumn and early winter *Molinea* grass still makes a show on the hillsides, turning silver as the leaves grow bleached and brittle. In early winter gales the leaves are carried on the wind, earning the plant its country name of 'flying bent'. Sometimes, fences and thorn-bushes are turned into miniature haystacks as they gather the flotsam of the wild pastures. Above the moor-grass and the bracken beds of the lower Cheviot slopes, mat-grass

The Cheviot from Windy Gyle on the Border ridge. An April shower has just hurtled through and the air temperature has crashed by ten degrees (with another ten for the wind-chill).

A Cheviot shepherd, Ambrose Anderson, at Ingram in the Breamish Valley.
He is holding a cross-bred lamb, whose mother is getting very angry.

takes over dominance. Its bleached stems again turn the winter landscape pale. The andesite of the Cheviots is 'white land': it is only on the granite core of Cheviot/ Hedgehope and along the poorly drained border ridge that heather, bilberry and crowberry appear in profusion.

Close to Ravens Knowe ('knowe' means rounded hill) is Ogre Hill, where the path touches the upper edge of the forest and meets the Scottish border. For the first time there are big views to the north, where the triple peaks of the Eildon Hills, above Melrose, catch the eye. Many of the most prominent hill tops in this part of Britain were settled in the Iron Age as hill forts: the Eildons are a dramatic example. When Agricola brought a Roman army north in the early years of the occupation he had a fort built at Melrose to keep the locals quiet and to act as a stepping stone for further campaigns. The fort was called Trimontium, the three peaks. The road by which his soldiers marched north from York was Dere Street; it climbed from Redesdale into upper Coquetdale, where there was a marching camp at Chew Green, then climbed again to Brownhart Law, where there was a signal station. It is possible to stand on Ogre Hill and make out the line of the road, and the complex earthworks of Chew Green. It is as wild a place now as it must have been in Roman times. After the windswept Cheviots it must have been a relief for legionaries to be heading downhill, to the comforts of Trimontium.

The Scottish border is marked by a ramshackle wire fence. In other circumstances this might seem a modest affair but on this featureless saddle of blanket bog it has been a reliable and steadfast friend to anyone heading north.

A sight rarely seen by Pennine Way walkers: sunset on the Border Ridge. Anyone caught out this late either has a long way to go in the dark or is carrying a tent.

The route of the Pennine Way follows the fence, and over the last decade the path has been stone-slabbed in most of the more boggy places. Thus the Way is fixed and firm; there is no longer any need to wander right or left to try and find a way over black ooze. A mountain refuge hut at Yearning Saddle is the only place for miles where it is possible to escape the prevailing climate for a moment and have a rest or an energy bar (which has replaced a fag as the recommended restorative). The weather is usually bad here. Sometimes it is dreadful; occasionally it is glorious.

Windy Gyle is perhaps the most recognised and remembered high point along the border ridge. Not only is it high, but it also has a clearly defined summit. It separates two cross-border paths called The Street and Clennell Street - both assumed to be drove roads, trade-ways and reiver routes, but probably prehistoric. The summit of Windy Gyle stands on the Scottish side of the border and is marked by a great pile of boulders called Russell's Cairn. Over the years people have cleared a scrape among the boulders to act as a shelter. Of all places along the Pennine Way this is one of the most eerie. The pile of stones dates from the Bronze Age, when the climate here was a little better and farmers were working the Cheviot slopes: this high hill would have been an ancestral beacon for them.

The name Russell's Cairn refers to Sir Francis Russell, Warden of the Middle March, murdered in 1585. Windy Gyle lay in the Middle March, a dangerous no-man's land where evil deeds were a matter of opinion and justice was dispensed at regular but secret Wardens' Meets.

This spare and lonely landscape owes its soul to troubled times: whilst most of the country was witnessing great adventures with seed drills and bobbing jennies, this was called The Waste. Yet it was to Windy Gyle that Tom Stephenson brought members of the National Parks Commission in the 1950s, when he was trying to convince them that the Cheviots should be part of Northumberland National Park. Clearly, we have learned to cherish our wild places.

Blackface ewe and lambs. This is still the classic sheep breed of the Cheviot's high heather country, though some farms run Swaledales instead.

The Hanging Stone, on the south-west shoulder of Cairn Hill, near where a path detours east from the Pennine Way to take in the Cheviot summit. The Hanging Stone is where the medieval East March met the Middle March: a place of dark deeds and betrayal in the Border Wars.

Clennell Street to Kirk Yetholm

Raven

The peat beds of the Cheviot uplands used to feature in walkers' nightmares. King's Seat and Auchope Cairn were notorious sections of the Pennine Way where any spark of appreciation of the wonderful landscape was extinguished in a malodorous slurry of peat. In truth the border ridge was not very different then from other stretches of the Way such as Kinder and Black Hill: the going was equally terrible. But for most people the high Cheviots came on the last day of a long walk, and when they were sharing their stories later in the bar of the Border Hotel, their memories dwelt on the most recent horror.

For many years there were discussions within the Countryside Commission about whether the infamous peat furrow should be consolidated in some way, by laying matting or by paving the route. Die hard ramblers in the Peak District wanted everything to be left as it was, but nobody who knew the Cheviots complained when the first pallets of sandstone slabs were helicoptered onto the border ridge in the early 1990s. Since then most of the bad sections have been rendered passable with lightweight boots. Travellers' tales at the Border Hotel now concentrate on the amount of weather encountered on their long fortnight's journey.

The high Cheviots receive over a metre of rainfall a year. This is about half the amount that falls on Cross Fell, but on the border ridge there is nowhere for the water to go; it is held in a thick peat bed over impervious bedrock. The climate of the Cheviots is also colder than further west and south: summers are short. This has led to the establishment of a sort of impoverished tundra vegetation, more like arctic Finland than the Alps. Bilberry, crowberry and cottongrass are the dominant plants, with

The Border Ridge on the climb east to Cairn Hill. The fence marks the international frontier.

heather on the drier sweeps of ground. In places there are drifts of cloudberry a pretty plant with white flowers and red (edible) fruits. On more neutral or mineral soils, mainly on the baked andesite crags around the granite dome of The Cheviot, there are rare alpine flowers like starry saxifrage, globeflower and roseroot. Taken as a whole, the flora of the Cheviots is poor compared with Teesdale or the Yorkshire Dales, but for walkers crossing the massif in October and November, the vibrant colours of the landscape are a special joy.

Trees are missing from the Cheviot uplands. It was not always so; in post-glacial times most of the hills were covered in a close-woven carpet of pine and birch, and by five thousand years ago, at the end of what is known as the Atlantic Period (a warm wet phase: Britain's 'climatic climax'), oak forests covered all but the highest ground. With high rainfall came peat formation, and strong winds and cooler summers then caused the primeval forests to descend below the 2,000 ft contour. However, it was farming that put paid to most of the wild wood in the Bronze Age; crops were grown on all the lower slopes and well up the

A busy day at the mountain refuge hut on the Border Ridge between Auchope Rig and Red Cribs. Every few years the Karrimor International Mountain Marathon takes place in the Cheviots, and for two days the hills are awash with high-speed orienteers.

valleys. When the climate got worse again in the Iron Age, and through to medieval times, there was some recovery of scrub-woodland, but this was cut down for fuel or as building material. In the border troubles, anything that could be stolen, including trees, was fair game.

In fact, the look of the land today owes a lot to the desperate days of the Border Wars. It is hard now to appreciate how bad the situation was in this part of Britain before the Union of the Crowns in 1603. Old documents provide some clues, and some local colour. Here is an extract

from a report from Warden of the March, Sir Robert Carey:

'On the 2nd instant a company of 200 Scots, 80 of them and more, armed with 'calyvers' and horsemens peeces' came into England, their purpose unknown to me. I made all the force I could, and sent

England's Big Country: the College Valley from Red Cribs. Most of the hills are topped by Iron Age hillforts.

Last mile along the way: Kirk Yetholm and the Bowmont Valley from The Loanings on the Halterburn road.

Edale and the Nag's Head seems a lifetime ago. A free half pint awaits anyone who has just finished the whole route.

with speed to encounter them. And about 3 PM Mr Woodrington and Mr Fenwick whom I sent as leaders, set upon the Scots within England, and overthrew them. They were then so near their own borders, that they had "recovered Scotland" before we got to them. But the foray being broken, they held on the chase two miles into Scotland and private men slew their enemies who were in deadly feud with them, as they came to them: so I think there are some 4 or 5 Scots slain, and 16 of the best taken prisoner. After our men made a retreat, the prisoners were asked what their meaning was to enter the Queen's dominions with such force in warlike manner? They said their only intent was to hunt, and take such venison as the country afforded... They knew quite well it was unlawful... But these men, though the chiefest of them have been great offenders to this March both in blood and goods, and that lately, chose to make this bravado. Besides their hunting, their custom is to bring in 100 men at these times, to cut and carry away wood and they have thus clean wasted "one of the goodlyest woodes" in the Middle March.'

Perhaps on a misty cold evening, having seen no one all day, it is not too difficult to

Fox moth caterpiller

imagine the Border Ridge as a dangerous place still. Names on the map like the Hanging Stone and Murder Cleugh add an extra shiver to the spine. Whether the Scots can be entirely blamed for stealing away the forests is doubtful; sheep have been ranched on the Cheviot Hills for over a thousand years and are responsibile for at least a share of the theft.

In recent years there has been a decrease in sheep grazing in the Cheviot Hills, and a rapid increase in grouse management. This has not necessarily made a difference to tree cover, but it has resulted in an improvement in the quality of heather moorland. It is easy now to come across the big hairy caterpillars of northern eggar and fox-moth, which like to sun themselves along the paths, and to catch a glimpse of tiger beetles and carder-bees. High lonely places are always special for birds of prey: you are more likely to see a merlin here than anywhere else in England, and peregrines now occur wherever there are suitable crags for nesting. However, the essence of the high country is solitude. Sometimes you can walk for several miles without seeing anything.

Because the Cheviots were left waste when the rest of the countryside was modernised in the eighteenth and nineteenth centuries, even the lightest traces of archaeology have survived. Bronze Age field systems and palisaded settlements can be traced in the turf of the lower hillsides; these would have been ploughed out in any other part of England. By stark contrast, in the Iron Age the rounded middle-ranking hills of the border area were often used as hill forts, their massive ringed earthworks and stone ramparts still visible for miles around as their makers intended. By keeping to the highest ridge, the Pennine Way does not pass very close to any of the major hill forts, such as Yeavering Bell, Humbleton Hill, Hownham Law and Great Hetha. But most are visible from a distance; scan the horizon and any imposing hilltop will probably be the site of a hill fort. Our modern eyes are attracted by the same magic that our ancestors saw in the land. But for them it meant more. The closest the route comes to a prime hill fort site is Ring Chesters, about two miles off the route as you are making the final descent into the Bowmont valley. Not the best time to be contemplating a sightseeing detour.

Having crossed the Cheviot massif anyone who has taken on the whole Pennine Way will have overcome the final challenge. There is no sting in the tail: after the exhilarating last stretch of the ridge, linking the summits of the Schil and White Law, the path turns west via Green Humbleton and descends by quiet green pastures and pretty hedgerows into Kirk Yetholm. The countryside is surprisingly soft here, though the village itself has few frills. Yetholm started life as a farming settlement and was a gate-town ('yett' = gate) at the time of the Border Wars. Hence the general utilitarian architecture (except for the odd-looking church, which is a Victorian concoction). For many years Kirk Yetholm was known as the home of the gypsies. The last Gypsy Queen, Esther Faa Blythe, died here in 1883 and Walter Scott based his character Meg Merrilies on a Yetholm woman, Jean Gordon. The wide village green no longer plays host to regular gypsy camps: it is too far off the beaten track.

The Border Hotel marks the finish of the Pennine Way. No pub in Britain can be so eagerly anticipated, sight unseen. Stepping over the threshold is a spiritual moment: a fulfilment. There is still a notebook behind the bar where walkers can sign themselves in before claiming a free half pint. No drink ever tasted so good. A comment in the 2004 volume of the book sums up the feelings of most walkers: 'Experience of a lifetime... but it was a bloody long way'. And so it will always be.

Don't hang up your boots...

Index